The Little Mac Book

Lion Edition

Robin Williams

Peachpit Press

Berkeley • California

The Little Mac Book, Lion Edition

©2012 Robin Williams

Peachpit Press

1249 Eighth Street
Berkeley, California 94710

510.524.2178 voice
510.524.2221 fax

Find us on the Web at **www.peachpit.com**
To report errors, please send a note to errata@peachpit.com
Peachpit Press is a division of Pearson Education

Cover design and production: John Tollett
Interior design and production: Robin Williams
Back cover photo: John Tollett
Illustrations of Url Ratz: John Tollett
Index: Robin Williams
Editor: Nikki McDonald
Prepress: David Van Ness
Proofer: Cathy Lane

ISBN-13: 978-0-321-77658-7

ISBN-10:   0-321-77658-5

10 9 8 7 6 5 4 3 2 1

Printed and bound in the United States of America

To my mother, Patricia Williams,
who made it possible,
and to my father, Gerald Williams,
who would have been proud.

Thank you!

Many, many thanks to John Tollett, Nikki McDonald, and David Van Ness!

Contents

1   A Map of Your Mac   1

The Desktop 2
The menu bar 3
Finder windows 4
Home and Favorites 5
    Your "Favorites" in the Sidebar 5
Keys on your keyboard 6

2   The Mouse or Trackpad   9

Never used a mouse before? 10
    One button or two? 11
Using a trackpad? 11
Moving the pointer 12
The tip of the pointer 12
Gestures 13
Clicking the mouse 14
Single-click 14
Double-click 19
Press 21
Press-and-drag 22
    Moving the mouse when you've run out of space 24
Hover 24
    Shift-click 25
    Command-click 25
    Option-click 25
    Control-click 25
    Shift-drag 25
    Option-drag 25
    Command-Option-drag 25

3   The Dock   27

All those icons in the Dock 28
Display item names 30
    The tiny blue bubble 30
Resize the Dock 30
Remove an item from the Dock 31
Rearrange items in the Dock 31
Put an item in the Dock 32
Magnify the icons in the Dock 33
Reposition the Dock 34
When a Dock item jumps up and down 34

4   Finder Windows   37

The basic window 38
Four window views 39
    Icon View 39
    List View 40
    Resize the columns in List View 41
    Apply an arrangement 41
    Column View 42
    Resize the columns in Column View 43
    Cover Flow View 44
Quick Look/Slideshow 44
The Sidebar 45
    Remove items from the Sidebar 45
    Add items to the Sidebar 45
Window buttons 46
    Close a window (red button) 46
    Zoom a window (green button) 46
    Minimize a window (yellow button) 47
    Minimize windows into application icon 47
Make your own folders 48
    Enlarge the icons or the text 49
    Clean up the icons 49

5 Menus & Shortcuts 51

Choosing a menu command 52
    Single-click, slide, single-click 52
    Press–hold–let go 53
Black vs. gray commands 54
Hierarchical menus 55
Ellipses in the menus 56
Contextual menus 57
    Two-button mouse for a right-click 57
Keyboard shortcuts 58
    Modifier keys and their symbols 58
    How to use a keyboard shortcut 59
    Single arrows or triangles on buttons 60
    Other menus 60
    Double arrows 60
    Color wells 61

6 Use an Application 63

Open an application 64
Open a blank document 65
    New vs. Open 65
I-beam 66
Insertion point 66
Delete (or Backspace) 68
    Delete characters 68
Spell checking 69
    Control spell checking 70
One space after periods 71
Adjust the linespacing 71
Select (highlight) text 72
    Replace highlighted text 73
Change fonts (typefaces) and type size 74
Alignment 75
Cut, Copy, and the Clipboard 76
Cut 77
Copy 78
Paste 79
    An example of the cut-and-paste process 80
Undo 81

Keyboard shortcuts 82
Delete or Clear and the Clipboard 82
Access special characters 82
Use real accent marks 83
Document windows 84

7 Save & Print 87

Save your document 88
Save regularly 90
Explore the saved versions 90
Duplicate a document 91
Duplicate a document the Apple way 91
Duplicate a document another way 92
Print your document 93
Add a printer to the list, if necessary 94
Page setup 96
Print specifications 97
Application-specific options 97
See a preview 98
Copies & Pages 99
Layout 100
Printer-specific options 101
Using the print queue window 102
Control your print jobs 102
Keep your printer icon in the Dock 105

8 Close, Quit & Trash 107

Close vs. Quit 108
Unsaved changes 109
Close a document 110
Quit an application 112
Shortcut 113
Force Quit 113
Quit applications upon Log Out,
Restart, and Shut Down 114
Trash a file 115
More ways to trash files 116
Remove an item from the Trash 117

9 Get Connected 119

You need an Internet Service Provider 120
You need a modem. 121
Step by step: What to do 122
Information you need before you start. 123
Getting ready to set up. 124
Use Network preferences 124
Set up your broadband connection. 125
Connect to the Internet. 127
Set the service order 127

10 Surf the Web 129

What are web pages? 130
What is a web address? 130
If you want to connect right now 130
What are links? 131
Resize the text on a web page 132
Go back and forth from page to page 133
Open a new browser window 134
Check the Dock 134
Enter a web address. 135
Shortcut to enter an address 136
Choose your Home page 137
Bookmarks 138
View Bookmarks in Cover Flow 139
Put a web page link in your Dock 139
Check out the Top Sites page 140
Search tools 140
Important Point Number One 140
Important Point Number Two 140
Search using Google 141
Use Reader mode to remove web page clutter . . 142
Make a Reading List. 143

11 Let's do Email

Let your Mac set up your account............146
Set up your account manually.................147
   *Add, change, or customize a Mail account.........*148
Mail...149
   *The Viewer window...........................*149
   *Write and send an email message *150
   *Use stationery *151
   *Check for messages *152
   *Tips for writing messages.....................*153
   *Tips for replying to messages.................*154
   *Customize the Viewer window.................*155
   *Conversations in your email window *156
   *Attach a file to a message....................*158
   *Download an attachment someone sent you........*160
   *Create a Note...............................*161
Address Book................................162
   *Add new names and addresses to Address Book.....*162
   *Add a name and address from Mail..............*164
   *Send email to someone from your Address Book.....*165
   Address an email message in Mail
      *using the Address Pane.....................*165
   *Make a group mailing list *166
   *Send email to a group mailing list.............*167
   *Have your mail read out loud to you.............*167

12 Other Useful Features 169

System Preferences. 170
 Desktop & Screen Saver 171
Aliases 172
 Make an alias 172
 Details of aliases 173
Search for files on your Mac with Spotlight 174
 Narrow the search 176
 Find types of files 176
 Spotlight in applications 177
Stickies. 178
Sleep, Restart, Shut Down, or Log Out. 179
Burn a CD or DVD with a Burn Folder. 180
AirDrop 181
Mission Control. 182
Spaces. 184
Exposé. 186
Dashboard: Widgets at your fingertips. 187

Index 189

Special characters. 201
Accent marks. 202

Introduction

The Little Mac Book used to be really little—way back in 1989. In 100 pages, it told you everything you needed to know. The Mac itself was also little in those days.

Over the years, as the Mac got bigger and more powerful, *The Little Mac Book* got bigger and heavier—it finally morphed into an 850-page behemoth, and that didn't even include information on iTunes, iPhoto, and the other cool Mac applications!

But here is a "little" book again with just the very basic information to get you started using your new Macintosh. Of course, being little means there is a lot less information! This book should get you started. When you feel the need to know more, check out *Mac os x Lion: Peachpit Learning Series*. Peachpit also has lots of other great books on individual applications such as iPhoto, GarageBand, and much more.

Here's to a Grand Adventure!

Robin

A Map of Your Mac 1

This chapter presents a very brief **overview of your Macintosh.** It provides a "map" of what you see on your monitor. In this chapter I'll give you the names of things, since it's hard to know if you need to understand more about the "Dock" if you don't know what the "Dock" is! Skim through this chapter to get the gist of what you see on your screen, then refer to the map when you need to know where you can find specific information about a particular area.

Your Mac is full of **icons,** or small pictures. Start noticing the different icons and what you think they are telling you. For instance, icons that look like manila *folders* really are electronic "folders" in which you can organize other files. Icons that look like pieces of paper are *documents* that you (or someone else) created. The icon that looks like an *address book* is a small application in which you can keep names and addresses. Watch for the visual clues that icons provide to tell you what they are and what they do.

And everything is a **file.** That is, you'll hear the term *file* referring to icons of every sort. It simply means any item on your computer that has a name. Your documents are files, folders are files, photographs are files, etc.

Don't worry—you really can't hurt anything, so poke around!

Mermaid Tavern

Mabel.rtf

TextEdit.app

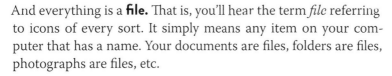

In this chapter

The Desktop 2
The menu bar 3
Finder windows. 4
Home and Favorites. 5
    Your "Favorites" in the Sidebar 5
Keys on your keyboard 6
Also Try This 7
Remember. 8

The Desktop

The **Desktop** is what you see when you turn on your Mac. It's like home base; you'll get to know it well. No matter what you're doing on your Mac, you can almost always see the Desktop, at least in the background (unless you're in a *Space;* see pages 184–185). The Desktop is just like an oak desk—you can spread all your "papers" out on top of it, and no matter what you're working on, the Desktop is always underneath it all.

This Desktop is also called the **Finder,** which is actually the software that runs the Desktop. Just consider them the same thing, home base.

There will always be a **menu bar** across the top of your screen. See the opposite page.

This is a **Finder window.**
See Chapter 4.

This shelf across the bottom of your screen is the **Dock.** Each of these icons in the Dock will open something when you single-click it. See Chapter 3.

These are your **Home** folders in the Sidebar, the folders you will use the most. See page 5.

This entire area is called your **Desktop.**

When you click the Desktop with the pointer, you are in the **Finder.**

Practically speaking, the terms **Desktop** and **Finder** are interchangeable.

The menu bar

As shown on the opposite page, you will always see a **menu bar** across the top of your computer screen. The items listed horizontally in the menu bar will change depending on what is "active," or front-most on your screen, as shown below.

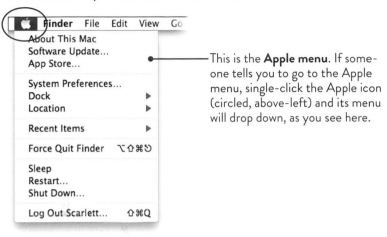

This is the **Apple menu**. If someone tells you to go to the Apple menu, single-click the Apple icon (circled, above-left) and its menu will drop down, as you see here.

Every **application** you open also has **its own menu bar.** Below, the open application is called "Preview," and you see its name on the left side of the menu bar. Notice this menu bar has different items from the one shown above. Start becoming aware of the menu bar! Notice how it changes when you open different files.

Under the **Application menu,** as shown below, the last item in the list of commands is always "Quit." Also, you'll always find the "Preferences" option for every application here in its own menu.

This is called the **Application menu** because it changes to show you which application, or program, is "active" at the moment.

TIP: You might someday play a computer game or watch a DVD movie and discover that you have no menu bar. Even if the menu bar is not visible, you can always press Command Q to quit. (See Chapter 5 for details on how to use a keyboard shortcut such as Command Q.

Or your application might be in full-screen mode where it fills the entire screen, in which case, push your pointer into the upper-right corner and a blue icon with arrows will appear; click it to return to the application on the Desktop.

Finder windows

You are going to become very familiar with **Finder windows,** as shown below. Essentially the *windows* represent *folders* full of *files* (see pages 1–2 if those terms don't make sense to you).

Now, it's possible to store files all over your Desktop, but that's just like storing everything in your office right on top of your oak desk. On your Mac, you'll get used to putting documents into folders and then opening those folders to view their contents in Finder windows. Chapter 4 gives you more details about windows.

Every window has a **title bar.**

The title in the bar tells you which **folder** you are looking inside of.

Every window has a **Sidebar.** The items shown in this Sidebar are all considered folders, even though their icons don't actually look like folders.

Single-click each item, each folder, in the Sidebar; its contents are displayed in the main window pane.

If you do not see this Sidebar, double-click the very left edge of the window to make it appear.

Every window **pane** displays the contents of the *selected* folder. This window pane is displaying the contents in **Icon View,** which you'll learn about soon.

In this case, you are seeing the contents of the folder called "Documents," as you can tell both by the name in the title bar and by the highlighted icon in the Sidebar.

Your Mac includes your own **Home** area with your favorite and private folders, your own Desktop, your own web bookmarks and email, and your own private Trash basket. Even if you are the only person using your Mac, you have an account with a Home folder—it was automatically set up for you when you turned on your Mac.

All the folders in the Sidebar belong to you, the user, and store your files. Until you have a good reason, don't change the names of any of those folders and don't throw any of them away yet. Later, you might want to learn how to create other user accounts on your Mac for your kids, your parents, visitors, or even for yourself.

The Sidebar displays the folders that are automatically created for you, the user, in the Favorites section.

All My Files: This folder displays all the files you have created or downloaded onto your Mac. You can't put anything in this folder yourself—they just appear here after you've created them (they're actually stored in your Documents or other folders).

AirDrop: You will see this in the Sidebar if your Mac is on a wireless network; use it to share files. See page 181.

Applications: This folder stores all the applications on your Mac. Its contents are also seen in Launchpad; see page 28.

Desktop: This folder holds the same items that are on your Desktop. If you get rid of a file on the Desktop, it automatically gets removed from this folder as well, and vice versa.

Documents: When you save your own documents that you have created, you can always find them in this folder (unless you have chosen to store them elsewhere).

Downloads: When you copy files from the Internet onto your computer, it's called "downloading." Also, when you get photos or documents in email or on disks, transferring those files to your computer is called downloading. Everything you download will automatically go into this Downloads folder. This same folder is in the Dock, next to the Trash, so no matter what you're doing, you always have access to it.

Movies: If you make digital movies in iMovie, your Mac will automatically store the files in this folder for you.

Music: When you use iTunes to buy music and make your own playlists, those music files are automatically stored here.

Pictures: If you use iPhoto, it will store your photos in here. You can also store photos in here yourself.

Home and Favorites

Your "Favorites" in the Sidebar

Keys on your keyboard

Your **keyboard** has a number of special **keys** that you will use all the time. Some of them are called "modifier keys" because they don't do anything when you press them down all by themselves—they only make something happen when used in combination with other keys or with the mouse.

Below are the keys you will become very familiar with, if you're not already. In Chapter 5 you'll start using keyboard shortcuts to do things on your Mac, and in that chapter I'll show you the symbols for each key that you see in the menus.

These first four keys are the primary modifier keys you'll use.

Shift key: This is the key, of course, that makes capital letters. It's labeled "shift."

⌘ **Command key:** This is the key on both sides of the Spacebar, with the cloverleaf symbol on it. Some people call this the "Apple key" because it used to have an apple symbol on it.

Option key: This is next to each Command key and is labeled "option."

Control key: This key is on the bottom-left corner of the keyboard, labeled "control" (on some keyboards there is another control key on the right, bottom). Be conscious of whether a direction tells you to use the *Command* key or the *Control* key!

You'll also use these other keys in shortcuts.

Spacebar: If you have ever done any typing, you know that the long bar across the bottom of the keyboard is the Spacebar and it makes the space between words. Occasionally it is also used in some keyboard shortcuts.

Caps Lock key: Push this down to type in all caps. You can still type the numbers when Caps Lock is down.

Escape key: This is in the upper left of your keyboard, labeled "esc."

Tilde key: This is directly below the Escape key, with the Spanish tilde character on it. It looks like this: ~

Arrow keys: To the right of the main keys you might have a little set of four arrow keys. In certain programs, the arrow keys will move selected items around the page.

Fkeys: These are the keys across the top of the keyboard. Many programs will let you customize what these keys do.

fn key: This "function key" is used in combination with Fkeys to maximize the possibilities on laptops.

Also Try This

You might be working on your Mac and then go have a cup of tea, and when you come back, **the screen is black.** Don't worry—it's okay! What happened is that the Mac noticed you weren't using it, so it put itself to sleep, or at least put the screen to sleep.

To get your screen back, just tap any key at all on the keyboard or wiggle the mouse back and forth.

You can control when the computer or the screen goes to sleep. In Chapter 12 you'll read about the System Preferences, and by the time you get to that chapter you'll feel comfortable with opening the Energy Saver preferences.

. . . . , , ...

When you're typing, avoid using **ALL CAPS** because not only is it harder to read than lowercase, but it takes up too much space, and it gives the impression you're shouting. If at some point you discover that EVERYTHING YOU TYPE IS IN ALL CAPS, you probably accidentally hit the "caps lock" key (that's funny—on the key itself, the words are in lowercase). It's on the left side of your keyboard, above the Shift key. Just tap the key one more time to turn off the Caps Lock.

Remember. . .

As long as you don't throw things in the Trash just because you don't know what they are, you really can't hurt anything on your Macintosh. So feel free to experiment all you want. As you work through the exercises in the following chapter, it's a good idea to start with the first one and continue on through because some of them are dependent on the previous one.

Remember that your Mac does exactly what you tell it, which means it's *your* responsibility to learn how to tell it what you want it to do!

Have fun!

The Mouse or Trackpad

2

The **mouse** is one of the most basic and important tools on your computer. The combination of a mouse and icons (small pictures) revolutionized the computer world and made the Mac so much easier to use than existing machines. This chapter walks you through how to use the mouse properly, and along the way you'll learn many of the **basics** of using your Mac in general. If you're new to the Mac, don't skip this chapter even if you know how to use a mouse!

Then again, you might have a laptop and will be using a **trackpad;** this chapter also covers the basics of using the trackpad. If you find you hate the trackpad, you can always plug in a wired mouse or "pair" a wireless mouse with your laptop.

Keep in mind, throughout this book, whenever I use the term "mouse" in reference to an action, it also refers to the trackpad.

In this chapter

Never used a mouse before?. 10

One button or two?. 11

Using a trackpad? 11

Moving the pointer 12

The tip of the pointer. 12

Gestures 13

Clicking the mouse 14

Single-click. 14

Double-click. 19

Press. 21

Press-and-drag. 22

Moving the mouse when
you've run out of space. 24

Hover. 24

Also Try This. 25

Remember. 26

Never used a mouse before?

In case you've never used a mouse before, below are guidelines, but today there are so many variations in the mouse that it's impossible to cover every possible instance. You must take responsibility for figuring out how to use your particular mouse!

- Keep the mouse on a flat surface, like your desk or table. That is, you don't need to point it at the screen or hold it in the air or touch it to the monitor. Just move it around on a flat, smooth, horizontal surface.

- If it has a cord, the cord should be facing away from you.

- Keep one finger positioned on the top end of the mouse where the cord (if there is a cord) connects. *The top of the mouse* is considered the mouse "button," even though you don't see an actual button.

  Now, if you have a mouse with an actual little button in the *middle*, like the one shown below-left, that is not the mouse button! Odd, isn't it? That thing that actually looks like a button is a "scroll wheel" that you can use to move around documents, web pages, lists, etc.

  When a direction tells you to "click" on something, push the left-front end of the mouse down. You will hear a "click" sound when you push in the right place.

- If your mouse has two "buttons," one on the left and one on the right, always use the left button unless the directions specifically tell you to use the right one.

- A mouse pad is a flexible little mat that helps gives your mouse traction, but it's not required. There's nothing magical about a mouse pad that makes a mouse work— you can use your mouse without any pad if you like.

- If you have a laptop that uses a trackpad instead of a mouse, see the following page.

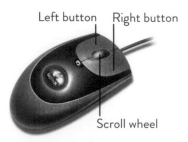

Left button   Right button

Scroll wheel

This is a two-button mouse where you can actually see both a left and right button.

This entire area is considered the mouse button.

This is Apple's Magic Mouse. Even though you don't see two buttons toward the top of the mouse, it is sensitive to a click on the left and on the right.

One button or two?

Most any mouse that you buy today has the top end divided into a left button (even though you don't really see a "button") and a right button, even if you can't see the division. Apple's Magic Mouse, for instance, shown on the opposite page, has one smooth surface, but you can use the left or the right buttons to do different things (mostly, contextual menus, as explained on page 57).

The default, however, on the Mac is that the right-click button is *not* turned on. This might be a good thing if you are new to the mouse because when both buttons are turned on, you have to be very careful where you click or unexpected things happen. So if you are just learning to use a mouse, leave it like it is for now. When you're ready, turn on the right-click (see page 170).

Using a trackpad?

A laptop has a built-in **trackpad** to do what a mouse does. The trackpad is a flat space on which you drag your finger to move the pointer around the screen. It takes a little time to get used to it. If you don't like to use the trackpad, you can always plug in a wired mouse or connect a wireless mouse instead.

- Move *one* finger around the trackpad.
  When you want to click on an item, tap the "bar" at the bottom of the trackpad (shown below).

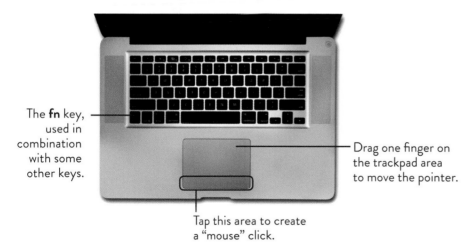

The **fn** key, used in combination with some other keys.

Drag one finger on the trackpad area to move the pointer.

Tap this area to create a "mouse" click.

There are several controls you can set for your trackpad that can make it easier to use, depending on how you like to work. When you get to Chapter 12, read about the System Preferences, then use the "Trackpad" preferences to change the settings for your trackpad.

Moving the pointer

As you move the mouse across the mouse pad or your finger across a trackpad, a **pointer** moves around the screen in the same direction as the mouse or your finger.

This is the pointer you'll see on your computer screen.

Once you start working in different applications, you'll see the pointer change into different shapes, sometimes generically called **cursors.** No matter what form it takes, the pointer or cursor will follow the mouse/finger direction as you move it.

If you feel like you're having to move your mouse or finger too far in relation to how far the pointer on the screen moves, you can adjust it: When you get to Chapter 12, read about the System Preferences and then use the "Mouse" or "Trackpad" preferences to make the "tracking speed" faster.

- Move the mouse around the mouse pad or your finger around the trackpad and watch the pointer until you feel comfortable moving your mouse/finger while looking at the screen.

The tip of the pointer

The only part of the pointer that has any power is the **very tip,** called the **hot spot.** When you need the pointer to activate something, be sure that the extreme point of the arrow is positioned in the area you want to affect.

This is the **hot spot** . . . .

For instance, in the exercises on the following pages you will click in the little red button of a window. Be sure to position the pointer like so:

Only the **very tip** of the pointer (the hot spot) does the trick.

If you have a Multi-Touch device such as an Apple Magic Mouse or Magic Trackpad (one that you can connect to your desktop Mac) or a new Mac laptop with the Multi-Touch trackpad built in, you can take advantage of **gestures** like *swipes* and *pinches* to make things happen on your Mac. If you've used your finger on your iPhone or iPad, you'll find gestures on the Mac work much the same way.

Gestures

For instance, if you have a Multi-Touch device, try this:

1   On a Magic Mouse, use *two* fingers and swipe from left to right. Swipe across the middle of the mouse, to the right.

   On a trackpad, use *three* fingers and swipe to the right.

   You should now see the Dashboard on your screen (explained on page 187).

2   To go back to the Finder screen, swipe to the left.

Open Mission Control:

1   On a trackpad, use *three* fingers and lightly swipe upwards, from the bottom to the top of the trackpad.

   On a Magic Mouse, use *two* fingers and lightly tap in the middle of the mouse.

   This puts you into Mission Control, as explained in Chapter 12.

2   To go back to the Finder screen, swipe three fingers down on the trackpad, or tap twice with two fingers on the mouse.

There are many gestures you can use to scroll up and down through a web page, or left and right to view different pages. You can triple-tap on a word to find its definition, rotate images with your fingers, and more.

To turn gestures on or off and to see little videos describing how to use them, use the Mouse or the Trackpad preferences; see page 170 on how to access the System Preferences and choose the Mouse or the Trackpad option, depending of course on what you're using. I suggest you start with one gesture and get comfortable with it, then add another to your repertoire.

Clicking the mouse

Separate from the *gestures* explained on the previous page, there are **four basic things** you'll do every day when working with files on your Mac:

- Single-click
- Double-click
- Press
- Press-and-drag

On these next few pages you'll go through short exercises to understand the differences between the techniques and when to use them. It's important to go through these exercises in order because each one requires that you did the one previous!

Single-click

A **single-click** is a quick, light press on the front end of the mouse, with the pointer (or other cursor) located at the spot of your choice on the screen; you'll hear a click. On a trackpad, lightly press near the lower edge of the trackpad (as shown on page 11) to make the click.

As you work on your Mac, these are the kinds of things you'll do with a single click:

- Single-click an icon on your Desktop or in a Finder window pane to *select* that icon.
- Single-click a menu to *display* its commands, as shown on page 18.
- Single-click an icon in the Sidebar of a window to *display* that item's contents in the window.
- Single-click an icon in the Dock to *open* that application or document.
- When you're typing, as explained in Chapter 6, you'll single-click with an "I-beam" to set down an "insertion point" for text.

Exercise 1: Use a single-click to select an icon on the Desktop.

- If you see an icon of your hard disk in the upper-right corner of your screen, **single-click** that icon. (If not, skip to the next exercise.)

  A single click "selects" an individual icon that is on the Desktop or inside of a window so you can do something with it. You're not going to do anything with it right now except notice it.

Robin's hard disk

This is a typical
unselected icon.

This is a Finder window. Tour

When you single-click an icon, the blue highlight is your visual clue that the icon/file is selected.

Note: To deselect an icon, click on a blank spot on your Desktop or inside a window.

Exercise 2: Use a single-click to open a Finder window.

- In the Dock (that bar of icons across the bottom of your screen), **single-click** the smiley icon on the left end, which is the Finder icon.

  When you single-click an icon in the Dock, it *opens* that item. In this case, you have opened what's called a **Finder window.**

  If you already had a Finder window open on your screen, nothing appears to happen except that window makes itself available to you. Continue to the next exercise.

This is the Finder icon in the Dock.

This is the **Sidebar** of a Finder window.

This is a **Finder window.** Your window might not have much in it yet, but soon it will be full of the files you create.

"Single-click" continued

Exercise 3: Display the contents of the Applications folder in the same Finder window.

- In the Finder window that opened in Exercise 2, **single-click** the "Applications" label in the **Sidebar.**

  When you single-click a label or icon in the Sidebar, that item displays its contents in the window pane to the right. These icons in the Sidebar are actually the equivalent of folders, in that they store other files for you. If your Mac is brand new, the "folder" in the Sidebar named Documents is probably empty at the moment—that's okay. Go ahead and single-click it to check.

The name in the **title bar** of the window tells you which folder you are seeing in the window pane below.

When you single-click an item in the Sidebar, the window pane on the right changes to display the contents of the item you clicked. For instance, here you see the applications that are stored in my Applications folder.

Exercise 4: In the same Finder window, change the view of the window pane.

"Single-click" continued

1 **Single-click** the **Documents** icon in the Sidebar.

2 **Single-click** the second button of the four **view buttons,** as circled below.

These view buttons let you see the contents of your window in four different ways: as icons, as a list, in columns of information, and as images. You can decide for yourself how you like best to view your windows. You'll work more with these different views in Chapter 4.

These are the four **view buttons:**
Icon View, List View, Column View,
and Cover Flow View.

The view button that is dark indicates
the currently selected view.
In this example, it's the List View.

"Single-click" continued **Exercise 5: You can always open a menu with a single click.**

1 **Single-click** in the title bar of your Finder *window* to make sure it is "active," or the front-most item.

2 Now **single-click** in the **menu bar** at the top of your screen, on the item named "View," as shown below.

3 Slide *down* the menu (*without* holding the mouse button down!) and **single-click** the command "Hide Toolbar." Watch what happens to your window—the Toolbar and the Sidebar both disappear.

4 Repeat Steps 1 through 3 and this time choose "Show Toolbar." (Also notice you can choose to change your window view from this menu *instead* of using the view buttons as you did in Exercise 4.)

This is the **menu bar** you see across the top of the screen when you are "at" the Desktop (or "in" the Finder—same thing).

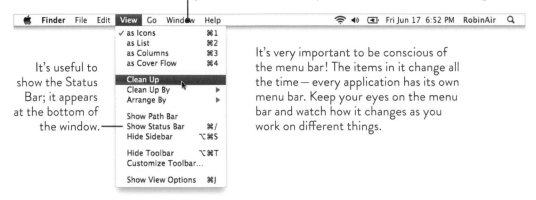

It's useful to show the Status Bar; it appears at the bottom of the window.

It's very important to be conscious of the menu bar! The items in it change all the time — every application has its own menu bar. Keep your eyes on the menu bar and watch how it changes as you work on different things.

Exercise 6: Close the window and go to the next exercise.

- **Single-click** the **red button** in the top-left of the window.

  Remember, you must position the *tip* of the pointer inside the red button before you click the mouse.

  If you accidentally click the *yellow button,* don't worry— all you did was "minimize" the window into the Dock (which we'll talk about in Chapter 4); just click the Finder icon in the Dock again to bring the window back.

  If you click the *green button,* it will enlarge or reduce the size of the window.

Single-click the **red button** in any window if you want to **close that window.**

Double-click

A **double-click** is a quick click-click on the front end of the mouse or the bottom of the trackpad, again with the pointer located at the appropriate spot on the screen. *A double-click has to be quick and the mouse must be still or the Mac will interpret it as two single clicks.* As you work on your Mac, these are the kinds of things you'll do with a double-click:

- Double-click an application or document icon to *open* that application or document (as long as the icon is not in the Dock or Sidebar —*single-click items in the Dock or Sidebar*).

- Double-click a folder icon (not in the Dock or Sidebar) to *open* the window for that folder.

- Double-click a word to *select* that word for editing.

- One day you will insert a CD or DVD disk. You'll double-click on that CD or DVD icon and its window will open. You don't have to do that right now if you don't have a CD or DVD available—just remember that it's a *double-click* to open its icon.

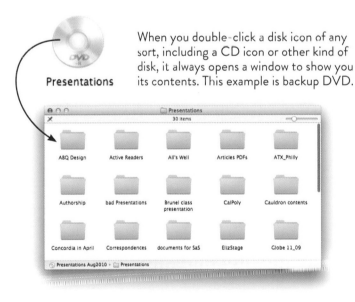

When you double-click a disk icon of any sort, including a CD icon or other kind of disk, it always opens a window to show you its contents. This example is backup DVD.

Presentations

"Double-click" continued **Exercise: Double-click to open a folder when a window is in Icon View.**

1 Your window should be open from Exercise 1 (if not, single-click the Finder icon in the Dock to open a Finder window).

2 If the Applications window is not showing, single-click "Applications" in the Sidebar.

3 Make sure the window is in Icon View, as shown below. (If it isn't, click the Icon View button, which is the one on the left of the four buttons, circled below.)

4 Type the letter U, which will select the folder named "Utilities," as shown above.

5 Now double-click that folder icon. It will "open" and display its contents in the pane, as shown below.

6 **To go back** to view the contents of the previous folder/ window, single-click the "Back" button, circled above left.

To **press** means to position the *tip* of the pointer on something and—don't click—*press* the mouse button or trackpad bar and *hold it down.*

Press

- Press items in the Dock to *pop up* their menus.
- Press the arrows in a scroll bar of a window to *scroll* through that window.

Often directions (not mine!) will tell you to "click" on things when they really mean "press." If clicking doesn't work, try pressing.

Exercise: Open the menus that pop up from the Dock (the shelf of icons across the bottom of your screen).

1 **Press** (don't click!) on an icon in the Dock.

   A little menu pops up (press and hold to the count of three, then you can let go and the menu will stay open).

2 To make the menu go away, click on a blank space anywhere on the Desktop.

This is the Finder icon.

Press on a Dock icon (don't click), and you'll see a menu. Different icons have different menus. To put the menu away, single-click on any blank spot.

Next exercise . . .

In a minute you can **scroll** through a window by pressing the scroll arrows. But first go to the following page and learn about press-and-drag so you can resize your window; otherwise there might be nowhere to scroll to!

Press-and-drag

In many manuals, this technique is misleadingly called **click**-and-drag.

Press-and-drag means to point to the object or the area of your choice, *press*/hold the mouse button down, *keep it down,* and *drag* somewhere, then let go when you reach your goal. On a trackpad, this means you need to hold the bar down with your thumb while you drag your finger.

- Press-and-drag to *move* icons across the screen.
- Press-and-drag to *move* a window across the screen.
- In a Dock menu, press-and-drag up the menu to *select* an item (then just let go when you select an item; don't click).
- When typing, press-and-drag to *select* a range of text.

Exercise 1: Move a window to a new position on the monitor.

1 If you have no window open, single-click the Finder icon in the Dock to open a Finder window.

2 With the *tip* of the pointer, *press* the title bar of a window, *hold* the mouse button down, then *drag* your mouse. This moves the window. Wherever you let go of the mouse, that's where the window will stay.

Exercise 2: Resize a window.

1 If you have no window open, single-click the Finder icon in the Dock to open a Finder window.

2 *Press* on any corner and drag that corner to resize the window. Or press on any edge and drag to resize.

Drag any corner to resize the window.

When a window is too small to display its contents, you need to scroll to see the rest. See Exercise 3.

Unfortunately, Apple turns off the scroll bars if you're using a Magic Mouse or trackpad, and they don't appear until you start to scroll. This means that in many views you have no idea if there are items you can't see. If you would like to have the visual clue of seeing the scroll bars (trust me, it comes in handy), see page 170 to turn them back on.

Exercise 3: Scroll through a window to see all the contents.

1 If you have no window open, single-click the Finder icon in the Dock to open a Finder window.

2 Single-click the Applications icon in the Sidebar to display the contents of the Applications folder.

3 Your Mac has more applications than can be seen in one window pane, so you need to scroll through the window.

With a Magic Mouse: With one finger, swipe upwards and downwards on the surface of the mouse.

With a multi-touch trackpad: With two fingers, swipe upwards and downwards on the surface of the trackpad.

With a wired mouse: You see a gray scroll bar on the side of the window; press-and-drag the gray bar up and down.

Using a multi-touch device, the scroll bar will appear as you swipe up and down.

To scroll sideways, as in the example below-right, position the pointer in the space and swipe left or right.

If your mouse or trackpad cannot use gestures (like a swipe), the scroll bar will appear so you can drag it.

With a wired mouse, when you need to scroll sideways and there is no scroll bar, as in the example above, *press* in the window and drag left or right.

Moving the mouse when you've run out of space

Sometimes you may be **dragging a file** across the screen and **run out of space** on the mouse pad or work surface before the pointer gets where you want it to go. Just do this:

1 Keep your finger on the mouse button, pressing it down.

2 Pick up the mouse, *keeping the button down,* and move the mouse over to where you have more room.

3 Then just continue on your path (with the button down).

This isn't a problem on the trackpad because your thumb will keep the bar down as your finger makes many numerous swiping motions to move the cursor across the screen.

Hover

There is one more mouse technique you might want to experiment with, called **hover.** Just position the tip of the pointer over a button or icon and hold it there—*don't click, don't press, just hover.* Often a tool tip or icon name appears, as shown below. Try it!

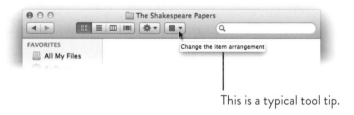

This is a typical tool tip.

Also Try This

Below are a few advanced uses of the pointer. You can skip this for now and come back when you see the term and need to know how to do it.

You will eventually see such terms as **Shift-click, Command-click, Option-click,** and **Control-click.** This means to *hold down* that key mentioned (Shift, Command, Option, or Control) and then click the mouse button once. Different things happen with each action. Try these:

- To *select* more than one icon in Icon View, Shift-click individual files. Shift-click also to *deselect* an item from a group of selected icons.

- To *select* contiguous files in Column or List View, single-click on a file at the top of a list, then Shift-click on the last file in the list that you want to select. All the files between the single-click and the Shift-click will be highlighted/selected.

- To *select* more than one file, or to *deselect* an item from a group of selected icons, Command-click individual file names.

- To get "contextual menus" (menus that offer different choices depending on what you Control-click, explained in Chapter 5), Control-click on various files, or on a window or the Desktop.

- To give you a menu choice to force an application to quit when it's acting stupid, Option-press that application's icon in the Dock.

You'll see directions like **Shift-drag, Option-drag,** or **Command-Option-drag,** which means *hold down* the Shift, Option, and/or Command keys and drag the mouse. Try these:

- To make a **copy** of a file, Option-drag a file from one window to another (or to the Desktop), then let go.

- To make an **alias** of a file (alias information is in Chapter 12), Command-Option-drag the file to another folder or to the Desktop.

Shift-click
Command-click
Option-click
Control-click

The Shift, Option, and Control keys are all labeled on your Mac. The Command key is the one right next to the Spacebar, with the cloverleaf symbol on it. See page 6.

Shift-drag
Option-drag
Command-
    Option-drag

Remember. . .

- When using the mouse or the trackpad, the **tip of the pointer** is the only thing that has any power! All the rest of the pointer is dead. So make sure the very tip is touching what you want to click on.

- When using a mouse, if you are in the process of moving the pointer and you **run out of room,** pick up the mouse, move it over, and keep going. If you've got the mouse button down because you're moving a file or dragging something, keep the button down while you pick up the mouse and move it.

- **Single-click:** Basically, single-click just about everything.

- **Double-click:** Generally, the only things you will ever double-click are file icons that are sitting on the Desktop or in a window pane, file icons that you need to *open,* such as document or application icons.

The Dock

The **Dock** is that strip of icons across the bottom of your screen; you'll find it to be one of your most important tools. In this chapter you'll experiment with using the Dock, adding icons to it and taking icons out, resizing it, and more.

If your Dock doesn't look exactly like this, don't worry—it is totally customizable!

In this chapter

All those icons in the Dock. 28
Display item names 30
   The tiny blue bubble 30
Resize the Dock 30
Remove an item from the Dock. 31
Rearrange items in the Dock 31
Put an item in the Dock 32
Magnify the icons in the Dock. 33
Reposition the Dock 34
When a Dock item jumps up and down. . . . 34
Also Try This. 35
Remember. 36

All those icons in the Dock

Below is a **description of each icon** that is probably in your Dock when you first turn on a new Macintosh. Don't worry if you have slightly different icons! An asterisk (*) under a number, shown below, means that icon will try to automatically connect to the Internet when you click it.

Dividing line

| 1 | 2 | 3 | 4 | 5 | 6 | 7 | 8 | 9 | 10 | 11 | 12 | 13 | 14 | 15 | 16 |
| | | * | * | * | * | | | * | | | | | | | |

1 Finder: Single-click the Finder icon when you need to **open a window.** If you did the exercises in Chapter 2, you are familiar with this icon and what it shows you (if you skipped those exercises, you might want to pop back to the previous chapter and run through them).

2 Launchpad: Single-click this icon to access all your applications. What you see in Launchpad is exactly the same as what is in your Applications folder, which you can access from the Sidebar of any Finder window.

3 App Store: Choose from many thousands of applications to download to your Mac, many of which are free. You'll need a credit card and an Apple ID, which you can create the first time you go the to App Store.

4 Mail: This is an **email** application to send and receive email. If by chance you have more than one email account (for instance, one for work and one for personal mail), Mail can check them all at the same time, and it can also send email messages from any of your accounts. See Chapter 11.

5 Safari: This is the software called a **browser.** It displays web pages, so this is what you'll use to surf, or browse, the web (see Chapter 10). If someone tells you to "open your browser" or "open Safari," this is what you'll click on.

6 FaceTime: With FaceTime you can video-chat with anyone else in the world who also has a FaceTime account—on a computer, iPhone, or iPad 2. FaceTime comes with Lion, but is also available in the App Store for a dollar.

7 Address Book: Collect and organize contact information such as names, addresses, phone and fax numbers, email, web addresses, birthdays, anniversaries, notes, and more. The Mail program can address your emails automatically using contact info from this Address Book. See Chapter 11.

8 iCal: Create and manage multiple, color-coded calendars of appointments, to-do lists, and important events. Set alarms for events. Automatically send and retrieve invitations for events, and if you have a MobileMe account from Apple, you can publish your iCal calendar on the Internet. We don't have room in this small book to provide details about iCal, but it's quite self-explanatory. Open it, double-click on a date, and enter your info.

9 **iTunes:** Transfer songs from music CDs to your Mac so you can play them without having to have the CD inserted into the computer. You can burn CDs of your own collections (called playlists); listen to radio stations over the Internet; and buy individual songs, entire CDs, audio books, college courses, and more right through the iTunes Store. We don't have room to provide details about iTunes in this book, but you can't go wrong by poking around in it!

10 **Photo Booth:** Use Photo Booth to snap photos or movies of yourself through your built-in camera or an attached digital video camera. You can email the photos, use them as your iChat icons, and more. Open Photo Booth, click the red button to take your photo, and play around.

11 **iPhoto:** Organize, label, find, and export your photos. Get Kodak prints made; create photo books, note cards, calendars; and much, much more. When you plug your digital camera in to your Mac, iPhoto will open and ask if you want to store your images in iPhoto. Be sure to click the "Create" button to see all the amazing things you can create with your photos!

12 **System Preferences:** The Mac lets you customize many of its features. For instance, you can change the picture on your Desktop, adjust your mouse, change the time zone, and more. See pages 170–171.

13 **TextEdit:** This icon probably isn't in your Dock, but you'll put it there if you follow the exercises in this chapter. TextEdit is a great little word processor for writing letters, lists, stories, or anything. See Chapter 6.

Dividing line: Every icon to the *left* of this dividing line represents an application, or program, that you use to do things with. On the *right* side, you can put your own folders and documents. And of course the Trash.

14 **Documents folder:** This is a copy of the Documents folder that is in your Home folder. Because it's in the Dock, it's accessible no matter what application you're working in. Click this folder to display its contents.

15 **Downloads folder:** This is a copy of the Downloads folder that is in your Home folder. It stores all files you have downloaded (copied to your computer) from the web, from email messages, or from anywhere else. You can move any downloaded folder to somewhere else, of course. Click the icon to display its contents.

16 **Trash:** Any file you don't want anymore you can just drag into this Trash basket. See Chapter 8.

There is just no room in this little book to explain how to use Preview, Photo Booth, iTunes, iCal, iChat, or Time Machine, but they are covered in the more advanced book written by me and John Tollett, *Mac OS X Lion: Peachpit Learning Series*.

The iLife applications you might have (iPhoto, iMovie, iDVD, iWeb, GarageBand) or iWork applications (Keynote, Pages, Numbers) are NOT covered in either book, but Peachpit has great books on every one of these applications. Please check their web site at www.Peachpit.com. There's so much to learn!

Display item names

You can "hover" the pointer (as explained on page 24) over an icon in the Dock, and a little **tooltip** appears that tells you the name of the item.

1   Without holding the mouse or trackpad button down at all, just position the pointer so the tip of the arrow sits on top of an icon in the Dock.

2   *Don't press the mouse button down,* but just "hover," holding the mouse still. A tooltip appears. It disappears when you move the mouse away.

This is a tooltip.

This technique is useful in many Mac applications. Try it whenever you see icons in a toolbar.

The tiny blue bubble

The tiny **blue bubble** you see under an icon in the Dock is an *indicator light* that tells you that particular application is open, even if you don't see signs of it anywhere. If you single-click an item in the Dock that has a bubble, that application will come to the front so you can work in it. (The Finder itself is always open.)

Resize the Dock

As you add and delete items from the Dock, the Dock gets **larger and smaller.** But perhaps you want it larger right now so you can see the individual icons better. It's easy to resize.

1   Position your pointer directly over the dividing line that is on the right side of the Dock. The pointer will turn into a double-pointy symbol when you are in the right spot, as shown below.

This is what the pointer turns into when you are positioned directly over the dividing line.

2   When you see the double-pointy symbol, press down the mouse button or trackpad bar and (keeping the button down) drag the pointer slightly, up or down. As long as the button is down, the Dock will resize as you drag.

If you find you never use certain applications whose icons are in your Dock, you can **remove the icons.** Don't worry—you won't destroy the original files! All you remove is the icon—you can't hurt the original application, folder, file, web site, or anything else.

You cannot remove the Finder icon or the Trash basket, though.

1 To remove an item from the Dock, press on it with the pointer.

2 Without letting go of the pointer, drag the icon off the top of the Dock and drop it anywhere on the Desktop. A cute little "poof" will appear.

This is the "poof" that appears when you remove something from the Dock.

To put an item back into the Dock or to put a *new* item in the Dock, see the following page.

You can easily **rearrange** the items in the Dock to suit your preference. Icons must stay on the side of the dividing line they are currently on, though—you'll find it's not even possible to move something from the right side of the dividing line to the left, and vice versa.

You cannot move the positions of the Finder icon or the Trash.

1 Press any icon in the Dock.

2 Without letting go of the pointer, drag the icon to the left or right as far as you want to go. You'll see all of the other icons move out of the way to make room for the one you're moving.

3 When you like the position, let go of the mouse button.

Here you can see the pointer is dragging the icon to the left.

You can drag up and over the top of the Dock, but be careful not to let go when the icon is out of the Dock or you'll delete it, as shown at the top of this page!

Remove an item from the Dock

If you don't use a digital video camera, you might want to take iMovie and iDVD out of your Dock (if they're there). When you need that application, put its icon back in the Dock.

Rearrange items in the Dock

If you accidentally delete an icon, see the following page for easy directions on how to put an item **in** the Dock.

Put an item in the Dock

To practice **putting an item in the Dock,** we're going to go to Launchpad and get the small word processor (an application used for typing letters or other documents) called **TextEdit.** You'll put it in the Dock so it's always available to you. You'll use this application in Chapter 6.

TextEdit

This is the TextEdit icon.

1 Single-click the Launchpad icon in the Dock (*or* you can click on "Applications" in any Finder window Sidebar to display the contents of the Applications folder.

2 Find the TextEdit icon.

3 *Press* (don't click!) the TextEdit icon and *drag* it down to the Dock; when the tip of the pointer is in the Dock, all of the other applications will move over. At that point, let go of the pointer.

Remember, you have to put an application on the *left* side of the dividing line.

Now the TextEdit application will always be in your Dock, ready for you to use it.

You'll notice that the TextEdit icon is still in Launchpad and in the Applications folder window, *plus* it is in the Dock. That's exactly as it should be—the Dock icon opens the real application that is always stored in the Applications folder.

You might like to turn on "Magnification" to **enlarge the Dock icons** temporarily as your mouse rolls over them. This is useful if you like to keep the Dock rather small but you want the icons to be bigger when necessary, or if you end up with so many items in your Dock that *everything* becomes very tiny.

Magnify the icons in the Dock

When "Magnification" is on, the Dock icons grow as you run your pointer over them.

1 Take the pointer up to the Apple menu, the black apple in the top-left corner of your screen.

2 Single-click the black apple to display the Apple menu.

3 Slide down to "Dock," then slide out to the right and single-click the option to "Turn Magnification On." The menu will automatically disappear after you do that.

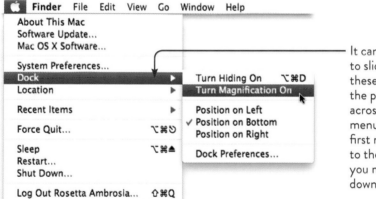

It can be a little tricky to slide out to one of these submenus. Drag the pointer straight across the highlighted menu command in the first menu, all the way to the submenu, before you move the mouse downward.

4 Now, down in the Dock, *do not click the mouse/trackpad button,* but just *slide* the pointer over the icons in the Dock.

To turn off this feature, repeat steps 1–3 above. The option to "Turn Magnification On" has changed into "Turn Magnification Off." Choose it.

Also see page 35 for a tip on how to turn magnification on and off from the Dock itself.

Reposition the Dock

You might like to position your Dock on the **left or right side of the screen,** instead of at the bottom. It's easy to do:

1 Take the pointer up to the Apple menu, the black apple in the top-left corner of your screen.

2 Single-click the apple to display the Apple menu.

3 Slide down to "Dock," then slide out to the right, then down, as shown below. Single-click the option to "Position on Left" or "Position on Right."

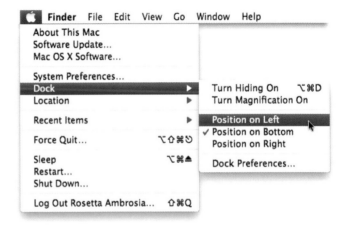

Of course, whenever you change your mind and want the Dock back at the bottom of the screen, just follow the directions above and choose "Position on Bottom."

When a Dock item jumps up and down

At some point you might see a **Dock item jumping up and down,** over and over, as if it's trying to get your attention. It is. This means that particular application needs you—click on the jumping icon and that application will "come forward" to become the *active* application. Then you will probably see a message on the screen that needs to be taken care of, such as "Do you want to save this document?" or "This application couldn't do what you wanted." Just do what it asks you to do.

This is different from the "bouncing" you will see when an icon starts to open (as you'll see in Chapter 6). The bounce is little; the jump is big. It's actually kind of cute.

Also Try This

Here are a few more advanced features of the Dock. You don't need to know these right away, so feel free to skip this page for now.

Hide the Dock. If you find that the Dock gets in your way, you can "hide" it. When hidden, the Dock slides down under the screen; when you shove your pointer down to the bottom of the screen, the Dock automatically slides up and stays there until you choose an item (or until you move the pointer higher). **To hide the Dock,** go to the Apple menu, choose "Dock," then choose "Turn Hiding On." Of course, to turn it off so the Dock is always visible, choose "Turn Hiding Off."

Enlarge the Magnification: Go to the Apple menu, choose "Dock," then choose "Dock Preferences...." If there is no check-mark in the tiny box next to "Magnification," click it. Then drag the slider to the right. The farther to the right you drag the slider, the larger the icons will grow as you run your mouse over the Dock, as explained on page 33. To put the preferences away, click the red button at the top left of the window.

Use the Dock menu: All of the commands you used from the Apple menu are also right in the Dock. To pop up the menu, hold down the Control key (not the Command key) and single-click directly on the dividing line in the Dock. Try it.

· ·

Force quit: If an application you're working in stops working, like the pointer is stuck or the little colored wheel spins forever, then you might have to **force the application to quit.** To do that:

1. *Hold down* the Option key and keep it held down while you do Step 2.
2. *Press* (don't click) the application icon in the Dock that's giving you trouble. This makes a menu pop up.
3. The last command in the menu is "Force Quit."
4. Choose that command, "Force Quit." That one application should quit, and the rest of your computer should be just fine. Open the application again and it should be good.

If your wired mouse or keyboard ever stops working, the first thing to do is unplug it and plug it back in again—that almost always kicks it into working.

Remember. . . .

- **Single-click** icons in the Dock to open them!
- **Press** a Dock icon to get its menu—try it.
- The tiny **blue bubble** beneath a Dock icon indicates that particular application is already open; single-click the icon to bring the application forward and work in it.
- Make the Dock work for you—reposition it, rearrange the icons, make it bigger or smaller, etc.
- If you want to know what a particular button or icon is or does, use the "hover" technique to display the tool tip, as explained on pages 24 and 30.

Finder Windows

4

A **Finder window** is a basic, fundamental element of your Mac. When you open any **folder** or **disk,** including your hard disk, the Mac displays the contents of the folder in a **Finder** window. This chapter walks you through a number of short exercises so you'll feel comfortable using these windows.

I assume you did the exercises in Chapter 2 so that you know how to click, press, press-and-drag, and maybe even Option-drag!

In this chapter

The basic window 38
Four window views of the same contents 39
    Icon View 39
    List View 40
       Resize the columns in List View 41
       Apply an arrangement 41
    Column View 42
       Resize the columns in Column View . . 43
    Cover Flow View 44
Quick Look/Slideshow. 44
The Sidebar 45
    Add items to the Sidebar 45
    Remove items from the Sidebar 45
Window buttons. 46
    Close a window (red button) 46
    Zoom a window (green button) 46
    Minimize a window (yellow button) 47
    Minimize windows into application icon . . . 47
Make your own folders 48
Also Try This 49
Remember. 50

The basic window

Below you see a **Finder window,** sometimes called a **Desktop window,** the kind you'll see when you open a folder or disk on the Desktop.

Later you'll work with a **document window,** the kind you'll see when you are using an application in which you create your work. The two types of windows are similar, but Finder windows have a few specific features.

When a Finder window is open and **active** (in **front** of any other window), the Application menu is always "Finder."

This is the name, or **title,** of the Finder window that is open. This particular window is called "All My Files" because the folder named "All My Files" is selected in the Sidebar.

This area at the top of the window is the **Toolbar.**

Single-click any item to display its contents in the window.

This area is the **Sidebar.**

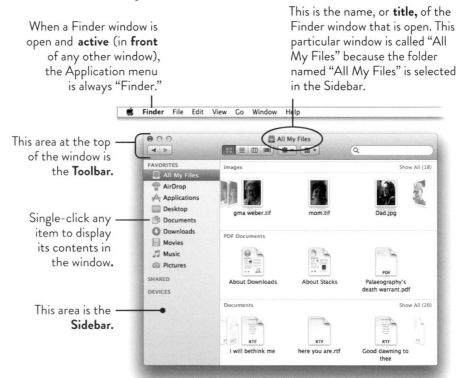

You can tell this is a Finder window because when you click on it, the menu bar across the top of the monitor, just to the right of the apple, shows the word "Finder." The Finder is the software that runs the Desktop, so all of the windows on the Desktop are considered Finder windows. Don't let that confuse you—just think of the Desktop and the Finder as the same thing, for all practical purposes.

The items inside a Finder window might be shown as icons, as a list, or in columns, as explained on the following pages.

You can change how you **view the contents** of a Finder window. Some people like to see their windows' contents as icons in **Icon View;** some prefer a list of names in **List View;** others prefer columns showing the contents of multiple folders at once in **Column View;** and some like the graphic **Cover Flow View.** In the short exercises that follow, you'll experiment with viewing the windows in different views.

Four window views

These are the View buttons in the Toolbar — click one to change the view of the "active" window (the window in front of all others).

Below you see a Finder window in **Icon View.** As you know by now, each icon represents a file of some sort—it might be a document, a folder, an application, a disk, a song, or something else.

Icon View

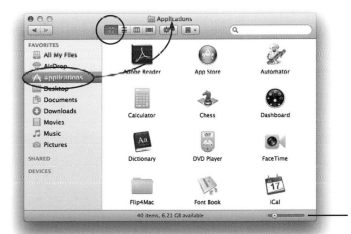

Icon size: Slide this dot to resize the icons.

If you don't see this slider, go to the View menu and choose "Show Status Bar."

Exercise 1: Experiment with views and with Icon View.

1 If you don't have a Finder window open, single-click the "Finder" icon (shown to the right).

2 In the Sidebar of the window, single-click "Applications." The contents of the Applications folder appear in the window pane, as shown above.

3 Now click the View buttons one at a time to see how the contents appear in each of the different views.

4 Go back to the Icon View: Single-click the far-left View button, as shown above.

5 When in Icon View, single-click another item in the Sidebar to view its contents. The view is probably different in another window.

6 Single-click "Applications" in the Sidebar to view the Applications window again.

Finder icon: Single-click this to open a Finder window.

List View · Below you see a Finder window in **List View.** Notice there are little triangles to the left of each folder icon. You can single-click any number of triangles to display the contents of folders. This way you can see the contents of more than one folder at a time.

Single-click the triangle pointing to a folder to display a sub-list of what is contained in that folder.

Or double-click a folder icon to display its contents in this same window.

Exercise 2: Experiment with List View.

1 The **List View** button (circled, above) is second from the left in the row of four View buttons.

2 When in List View, single-click any "disclosure" triangle next to a folder to display its contents in a sub-list in this same window.

You can open more than one folder in this way; try it.

3 **To see the contents of just one folder,** double-click any folder icon; the contents of that folder you double-click will *replace* the contents you see at the moment.

4 **To go back** to the previous window pane of contents, single-click the Back button, the triangle in the upper-left corner of the Toolbar.

Use the **Back** and **Forward buttons** to go back and forth between windows you previously opened.

Exercise 3: Resize the columns in List View to suit yourself.

Resize the columns in List View

1 Position the pointer directly on the dividing line between columns of information. When you are positioned correctly, the pointer changes into a two-headed arrow, as shown circled below.

2 When you see the two-headed arrow, press-and-drag left or right to resize the column. The column to the *left* of the two-headed arrow is the one that will be resized.

Exercise 4: Arrange the items in List View to suit yourself.

Apply an arrangement

When an *arrangement* is applied to a window, it organizes things in a particular way, but it also limits what else you can do. For instance, you can't resize or rearrange the columns or the items in the window. An arrangement can be a great solution for a window; just be aware of how it impacts other features.

1 From the *Arrange by* menu, circled below, choose an arrangement.

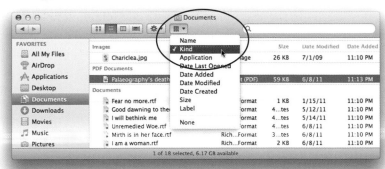

2 This can be very useful, but notice that you cannot resize the columns, nor rearrange them (by dragging the column names left or right).

3 Change the arrangement to "None" for now. Then try dragging a column heading left or right to rearrange it. The "Name" column cannot be moved.

Notice the difference between the two windows in Icon View on pages 38 and 39; the window on page 38 has an arrangement applied.

41

Column View

Below is a Finder window in **Column View.** Notice there are little triangles to the *right* of each folder icon. The triangles indicate that the contents of those folders will appear in the column to the *right* when you single-click the folder name.

The name in the **title bar** is the name of the **selected folder** (not the name of the document that may be selected **within** that folder).

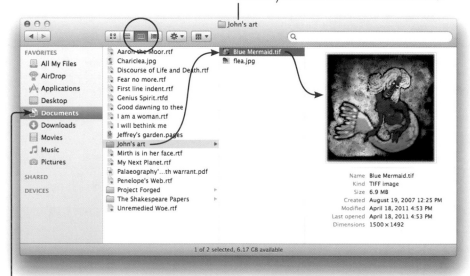

The **"Documents" folder** is selected, so its contents are shown to the right.

"John's art" folder is selected, so its contents are shown to the right.

A **file** is selected, and a preview is shown to the right.

If this file is a document with many pages, or if it is a movie clip or presentation or music file, you can play the movie, watch the presentation, listen to the music, or skim through the document pages, right here in Column View.

Exercise 5: Experiment with Column View.

1 Single-click the Column View icon in the Toolbar, as circled above.

2 Single-click "Applications" in the Sidebar.

3 In the first column of files, single-click any folder icon to see its contents displayed in the next column.

 If you see another folder to the right, single-click that one to display its contents in yet another column.

 Your Mac will keep making columns to the right until you select a *document* of any type (as opposed to a *folder*) or an application *package,* at which point a small preview will be displayed in the last column.

You can **resize the columns** in Column View using the vertical column dividers. Position the pointer on top of a dividing line, and the pointer changes shape to indicate it will now adjust columns.

Resize the columns in Column View

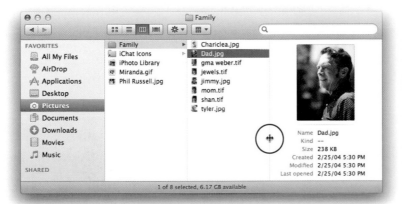

If you're using a mouse that cannot use gestures, you'll see scroll bars on the dividing lines and at the bottom of the lines, little "thumb" marks. Position the cursor on the thumb mark to follow these directions.

Drag to resize **one** column, the column to the left.
Option-drag to resize **all** columns.
Double-click to resize **one** column so the text is fully displayed.
Option–double-click to resize **all** columns to all text is displayed.

Exercise 6: Resize the columns in Column View.

1. **To resize one individual column at a time,** just press-and-drag left or right on any divider. This resizes the column to the *left* of the selected divider.

   If you're using a wired mouse, drag the thumb marker.

2. **To resize all columns at once,** hold down the Option key while you drag the divider or the thumb marker left or right. This makes *all* columns proportionally larger or smaller as you drag.

3. This is the most useful technique of all: Double-click on the dividing line or thumb marker to **widen the column so you can see the complete file names of all files.**

   This window in Column View has an arrangement applied, by "Kind."

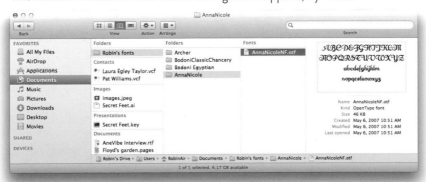

43

Cover Flow View

Below you see a Finder window in **Cover Flow View.** This is quite different from the other views in that it shows you a graphic image of each item in a folder.

- To skim through the images in the upper preview, use one finger to swipe across a Magic Mouse, or two fingers to swipe across a trackpad. With a non-gesture mouse, "press-and-toss" on either side of the center image to flip through them (try it!), or drag the slider that appears beneath the images.

Quick Look/ Slideshow

The Spacebar on your keyboard acts as a **Quick Look/Slideshow** button, showing you an instant preview of any file. Select an icon (click it once), then tap the Spacebar.

You can show an instant preview of a document, even if the selected file contains multiple pages. If you you select more than one item, you'll see slideshow buttons (left and right arrows) to go back and forth between documents.

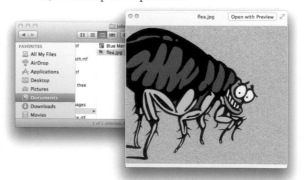

Exercise: Experiment with Quick Look/Slideshow.

1 Single-click an icon.

2 Tap the Spacebar to view it.

3 To view another file, single-click it, or select several files.

4 To put the Quick Look away, tap the Spacebar again or click the **X** in the upper-left corner of the preview.

The Sidebar

You have used the **Sidebar** a number of times already. Here are a couple of extra tips, as well as a press-and-drag practice.

Remove items from the Sidebar

You can **remove any item** from the Sidebar. This doesn't destroy anything! You are only removing an icon that *represents* the original file—you are not deleting any original files at all.

Exercise: Delete an item from the Sidebar.

- To remove any item from the Sidebar, hold down the Command key and drag the item to the Desktop. It disappears in a puff of smoke, as shown below.

Add items to the Sidebar

You can **add other items to the Sidebar.** You might want to add files or folders that you use the most often. You might want to put a current project folder here or, if your Dock is getting over-crowded, a favorite application.

1 Find the item that you want to add to your Sidebar.

2 Drag that item's icon to any position under the "Favorites" heading (you aren't allowed to put it anywhere else).

As you drag an item to the Sidebar, a blue, horizontal line appears. This line indicates where the item will be placed when you let go. If this isn't where you want it to be placed, drag up or down in the list until the horizontal line is in the position you want.

Window buttons

In the upper-left corner of each window are **three little buttons: red, yellow,** and **green.** These are in color in the *active* window (the one in front) and gray in all other windows behind that one.

From left to right, the buttons Close, Minimize, and Zoom.

When the pointer is positioned near the buttons, tiny symbols appear inside the buttons.

Close a window (red button)

Use the **red button,** the Close button, to **close a window.**

1 If you don't have a window open, single-click the Finder icon in the Dock to open one.

2 To close the window, single-click the red button. This puts it away, back into the folder or disk it came from.

Zoom a window (green button)

Use the **green button,** called the Zoom button, to zoom a window **larger or smaller.** How large or small the window becomes depends on what is in the window and how large or small it was before you clicked the button.

1 If you don't have a window open, single-click the Finder icon in the Dock to open one.

2 Single-click the green button to zoom the window large enough to see everything, or to zoom it smaller.

When you **minimize a window,** you send a tiny icon of that window down to the Dock, to the *right* side of the dividing line. Whenever you want to see that particular window again, you can open it straight from the Dock.

Exercise 1: Minimize the window and open it again.

- Single-click the **yellow** button to **minimize** the window, which sends the window down into the Dock, as shown below.

Useless-But-Fun Tip: To minimize an open window in slow motion, hold down the Shift key when you click the yellow button or when you click a window icon in the Dock.

This is the minimize button.

When a window is minimized, it floats down into the Dock as an icon, out of the way until you need it again. When you want it back, simply single-click its icon.

- **To open a minimized window,** single-click its icon in the Dock.

If you're feeling comfortable with minimizing windows, try this— make minimized windows hide behind the application icon in the Dock so they don't take up space. Just set this preference, below, and then watch the windows minimize behind their Dock icons.

Minimize windows into application icon

Exercise 2: Minimize windows into application icons.

1 From the Apple menu, choose "System Preferences…."

2 Single-click the "Dock" icon.

3 In the pane (shown to the right), check the box to "Minimize windows into application icon."

4 Close the preferences (click the red button, upper left).

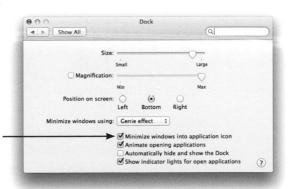

Make your own folders

You can make as many folders as you need to organize your files, and you can move the folders, put files inside of them, take files out, rename the folders, etc.

Exercise 1: Create your own folder.

untitled folder

Mermaid Tavern

1 Open the Finder window in which you want the new folder to appear; for instance, open the Documents folder.

2 Go to the File menu and choose "New Folder," **or** press Command Shift N.
A new folder appears in the selected window (or on the Desktop, if no window was selected).

3 While the new folder is highlighted, type its name. Click any blank spot on the screen when you're finished.

Exercise 2: Rename a folder.

1 Single-click the folder to select it.

untitled folder

This folder is highlighted, or selected.

2 Hit the Return or Enter key (or single-click directly on the name) to highlight the name.

untitled folder

This folder is ready for a new name. You can tell because there is a **border** around the name.

3 Type to replace the existing name. (You don't need to delete the original name first.)

Mermaid Tavern

Use the Delete key to backspace and delete characters or typos.

4 Hit Return or Enter to set the name, or just click in any blank spot in the window or Desktop.

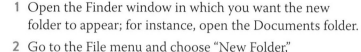
Mermaid Tavern

- **To put files into a folder,** press-and-drag the file over to the folder; when the folder highlights, let go.
- **To move a folder,** just drag it into another window or drop it onto another folder.

Also Try This

You can **customize** many things about the windows. Each view has its own options for customizing. When you're ready, check these out.

To change a window's **View Options,** click a Finder window, then go to the "View" menu and choose "Show View Options."

If the selected window is in Icon View, the pane shown on the right opens. *The options shown in this pane are different when the selected window is in List View or Column View;* check them out.

- Drag the **Icon size** slider to make icons larger or smaller.

- Resize the text names under icons with the **Text size** pop-up menu: Single-click the little menu bar (the one that now says "12"), then single-click a larger or smaller number.

- Choose a **Label position** of "Right" if you want to make icon labels (names) display to the right of icons instead of centered below them.

These icons have their labels on the right instead of at the bottom.

- The changes you make will affect only the *open* window. If you want these changes to apply to all windows in this view, click the button at the bottom to **"Use as Defaults."**

- **To put the View Options away,** single-click the tiny round button in the upper-left corner of the title bar.

If your folder full of icons starts looking messy, experiment with the options in the View menu: "Clean Up" and "Arrange By." Remember that an "arrangement" forces items into specific places and doesn't allow any flexibility; if you find you have trouble moving files into certain places, check to see if an arrangement has been applied. If so, choose an arrangement of "None," and you will be able to move files wherever you want.

Enlarge the icons or the text

Close button.

The title bar (circled above) displays the name of the **selected window.**

Clean up the icons

Remember. . .

- You will eventually figure out which **view** you like best for your windows. You might discover that you like some windows best in a list and some as icons, and sometimes you'll want to switch into Column View or Cover Flow View.
- Everything in a Finder window uses a **single click,** *except* when you want to *open* a folder icon into its own window pane.
- Make your own folders to keep your files organized.

Menus & Shortcuts

5

As you work on your Macintosh, you'll see a **menu bar** across the top of the screen, as shown below. Also shown below is a **menu:** When you single-click a word in the menu bar, a list of *menu commands* drops down. This chapter discusses various sorts of menus, the commands, and how to use them.

In this chapter

Choosing a menu command	52
Single-click, slide, single-click	52
Press—hold—let go	53
Black vs. gray commands	54
Hierarchical menus	55
Ellipses in the menus	56
Contextual menus	57
Two button mouse for a right-click	57
Keyboard shortcuts	58
Modifier keys and their symbols	58
How to use a keyboard shortcut	59
Also Try This	60
Other menus	60
Double arrows	60
Single arrows or triangles on buttons	60
Color wells	61
Remember	62

Choosing a menu command

There are two ways to **choose a command** from a menu. Both are explained below.

The method used in Exercise 1 is basically *single-click, slide the mouse, then single-click.*

The method you'll practice in Exercise 3 is *press-and-hold, then let go.*

Single-click, slide, single-click

Exercise 1: Display and put away menus.

1 Single-click any of the choices along the menu bar at the top of the screen. The menu pops open for you.

2 As you did in Chapter 2, slide the pointer (don't *press* the mouse/trackpad button down!) along the menu bar horizontally, and you will see each menu drop down.

3 On one of the menus, slide the pointer down the list of commands (don't *press* the button down). As the pointer passes over the different choices, each one *highlights,* or becomes selected.

4 **To put the menu away** *without* selecting a command, slide the pointer off to the side and single-click a blank area of the Desktop.

Exercise 2: Choose a menu command.

If there is no Finder window open, single-click the Finder icon in the Dock.

1 Single-click any blank spot in the Finder window to select that window.

2 **Single-click** the "View" menu name in the menu bar.

3 There is a checkmark next to one of the first four items in the View menu, indicating the chosen view for that particular window. **Slide** your pointer down the menu and **single-click** a different view.

Notice the menu disappears as soon as you click, and the view of the window has changed.

Choose another view for your window.

Some menus pop up, not with a single-click, but with a *press-and-hold-for-two-seconds.* Different menus might pop up depending on whether you click or you press-and-hold.

Press–hold–let go

In the Dock, for instance, you already know that a single-click *opens* that Dock item. But if you *press-and-hold* on a Dock item, you get a *menu.* One of the options is to "Show All Windows," which displays all the open windows belonging to that application on which you clicked.

Exercise 3: Open the Dock menu.

1 **Press** any icon in the Dock; *keep the mouse button down.*

2 A Dock menu pops up, as shown below. You don't need to choose anything right now—this is just an exercise so you'll know how to do it when necessary.

3 To put a Dock menu away, just **drag** your mouse off of the menu and **let go.**

What you see in any Dock pop-up menu depends on the item on which you click and what you have been working on in that application.

Black vs. gray commands

In a list of menu commands, some **commands** are in **black** letters and some commands are in **gray.** When a command is gray, it means that particular command is not available at that moment.

The most common reason a command is unavailable is because you did not *select* something *before* you went to the menu. For instance, you cannot choose "Open" from the File menu until you *select* a folder or file as the item to be opened. You cannot "Duplicate" a file unless you first *select* the file you want to duplicate.

Rule Number One
(Save Often, Sweetie)
is on page 88.

Rule Number Two on the Mac is this: **Select first, then do it to it.** Typically you select something with a single click.

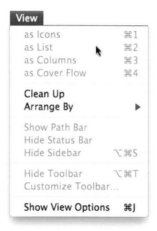

Some commands are gray; some are black. In this example, the different views are gray because no window is selected. If no window is selected, the Mac has no idea what to do with those commands.

This is the same menu as shown to the left, but this time I selected a window. Now I am able to change the view of the selected window.

Exercise 1a: Check the commands in the View menu.

1 Single-click a blank area on the Desktop so nothing is selected, not even a folder or window.

2 Single-click on the "View" menu and notice how many items are gray and thus unavailable.

Exercise 1b:

1 If a Finder window is not open, open one now (single-click the Finder icon in the Dock).

2 Single-click anywhere in a Finder window to *select* it.

3 Single-click the "View" menu and notice how many items are now black and available.

In some programs the menu itself contains a pop-out menu where you not only slide down, but also out to the side, usually in the direction of the arrow. These are known as **hierarchical menus, h-menus,** or **submenus.**

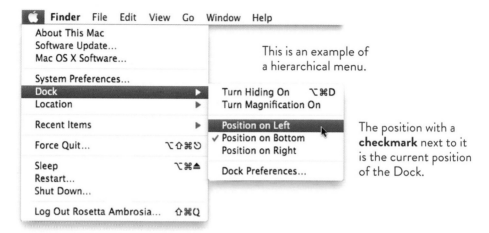

This is an example of a hierarchical menu.

The position with a **checkmark** next to it is the current position of the Dock.

Exercise: Use a hierarchical menu.

1 Single-click the Apple menu, as shown above.

2 Slide down to "Dock." Notice it has an arrow to its right, indicating it has a hierarchical menu.

3 Slide your mouse right *across* the blue line (it can be tricky!) until you get to the submenu, then slide *down.*

4 Single-click a different position for your Dock.

To put your Dock back where you want, repeat the steps above and choose the position you like best.

Ellipses in the menus

Often you will see an **ellipsis** (the three dots**...**) after a menu command such as "Open**...**" or "Save**...**." The ellipsis indicates that you will get a **dialog box** when you choose that command. *If there is no ellipsis, that command will activate as soon as you select it.*

There are different varieties of dialog boxes, such as alert boxes, message boxes, and edit boxes, plus dialog "sheets" that drop down from the title bar, but basically they all are meant to communicate with you *before* they activate a command.

A good dialog box will give you a **Cancel** button to make sure that anything you touched will not actually go into effect. If there is no Cancel button, click the **red close button** in the upper left of the window, or click the blue "Done" button.

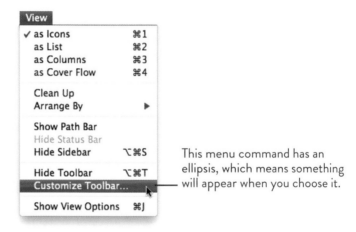

This menu command has an ellipsis, which means something will appear when you choose it.

Exercise: Experiment with ellipses in menus.

1 Open a Finder window, if one isn't already open (single-click the Finder icon in the Dock). Single-click anywhere on the window to make sure it is *active,* or *selected.*

2 Single-click the "View" menu.

3 Notice the command "Customize Toolbar…" has an ellipsis, as shown above. Single-click this command.

4 From the selected window, a "sheet" drops down out of the title bar. Pretty cute, huh? Play around with the options in this sheet.

5 When you're finished, single-click the blue "Done" button.

All over your Mac you'll find what are called **contextual menus,** menus that vary depending upon what you click on. You'll find different contextual menus in different icons, on a blank spot inside a window, a blank spot on the Desktop, in different applications, etc.

To get a contextual menu, hold down the Control key (the key in the far-left or far-right corner of the main part of the keyboard), then click anything and see what pops up.

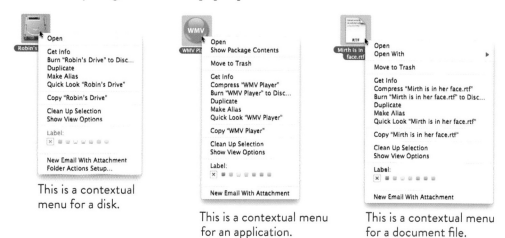

This is a contextual menu for a disk.

This is a contextual menu for an application.

This is a contextual menu for a document file.

Exercise: Use contextual menus.

1 Hold down the **Control key** and click a folder, *or* a blank spot in a window, a disk icon, a document, *or* an application.

2 For now, just take a look at the options in the different contextual menus.

3 **To put away a contextual menu,** let go of the Control key and click an empty spot on the Desktop or in a window.

If you have a **two-button mouse,** you can use the right-hand button to open contextual menus *without* holding down the Control key! Try it. Directions will tell you to "right-click."

If you have a mouse that is *supposed* to be two-button but it doesn't seem to be working, go to the System Preferences (from the Apple menu; see page 170) and choose "Mouse." Put a check in the box for "Secondary click."

Keyboard shortcuts

To the right of the commands in the menus you often see a little code, such as ⌘N (pronounced "Command N"). This is a **keyboard shortcut** you can use *instead* of using the menu. You memorize the shortcut, then the next time you need that command, you use the shortcut *instead* of picking up your mouse and pulling down the menu.

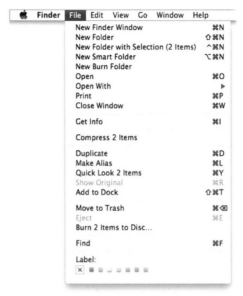

Often a keyboard shortcut includes other symbols representing other keys besides the Command key, as described below.

Modifier keys and their symbols

A **modifier key** is a key that doesn't do anything when you press it all by itself. For instance, when you press Shift, nothing happens; when you press the Command key, nothing happens. A modifier key makes *other* keys perform special functions. For instance, when you hold down the Shift key and type the number "8," you get an asterisk (*).

These are the **symbols** that represent the keys you will see in the menus for shortcuts.

⌘ Command key   ⇧ Shift key

⌃ or ⌃ Control key   ⌥ Option key

↺ Escape key   F1–F15 Fkeys

⇢ ⇠ ↑ ↓ Arrow keys   ⌫ Delete key

⇞ PageUp key   ⇟ PageDown key

To use a keyboard shortcut instead of the menu command, hold down the **modifier key** or **keys** you saw in the menu. While you *hold down* this key or keys, type the **letter key** you also saw in the menu—*just **tap** the letter, **don't** hold it down!* The computer reacts just as if you had chosen that command from the menu.

How to use
a keyboard shortcut

For instance, if you single-click a file to select it and then press ⌘O, the selected file opens just as if you had chosen that command from the File menu with the mouse. Thoughtfully, many of the keyboard shortcuts are alliterative: ⌘ **O o**pens files; ⌘ **P p**rints; ⌘ **D d**uplicates a selected file; ⌘ **W** closes **w**indows; etc.

You'll often see keyboard shortcuts spelled out with a hyphen, a plus sign, or perhaps a comma between the keys. **Don't type** the hyphen, plus sign, or comma! Just press the keys!

For instance, if you see a shortcut written as:

Command + Shift + B

ignore the plus signs—just *hold down* the Command and Shift keys (because they are both modifiers), then *tap* the letter B.

Exercise 1: Use a keyboard shortcut.

1 Single-click the "File" menu in the Finder. Notice that Command **N** is the shortcut to create a **n**ew Finder window, and Command **W** closes a **w**indow.

Single-click the Desktop to put the File menu away.

2 If there is no Finder window open on your Desktop, single-click the Finder icon in the Dock.

Once there is a Finder window open, single-click the window to select it (remember, commands only work on *selected* items).

3 *Hold down* the Command key and *tap* the letter W once. The selected window will close.

Exercise 2: Use more keyboard shortcuts.

1 You already learned that to make a new Finder window, the keyboard shortcut is Command N (N for New, of course). So simply hold down the Command key and tap the letter N once.

2 To make more Finder windows, hold down the Command key and tap the letter N several times in a row.

3 **To close all open windows,** use Command Option W: hold down both the Command *and* Option keys, then tap the letter W just once.

Also Try This

Other menus   You'll find other menus in all kinds of odd places. Well, they won't seem so odd once you become accustomed to the **visual clues** that indicate a menu is hiding. In the dialog box below, can you see the menus?

Double arrows   **Double arrows** are one visual clue that a dialog box contains a menu. Whenever you see that double arrow, as shown below, you can click anywhere in that horizontal bar and a menu will pop up or down.

Do you see the three menus in this dialog box? You can recognize them by the double arrows.

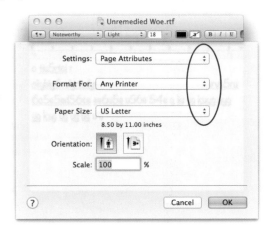

Single arrows or triangles on buttons   A **single** downward-pointing **arrow** or a **triangle** in a button all by itself *is not* a menu! This is called a **disclosure triangle** and typically expands a dialog box to present more information, as shown above-right, on the opposite page.

The fact that this information is hidden indicates that it is not necessarily critical at all times—you only pop open that information when you need it. As you are learning to use your Mac, click that arrow or triangle whenever you see it so you become familiar with the options, whether you use them or not.

On the opposite page is a typical dialog box in which you'll save your new document with a name. The **default** (the automatic choice that Apple makes for you) is to save your document in the folder called "Documents." This is perfectly fine. But if you'd rather save the file into a ***different*** folder, click the disclosure triangle and find the folder of your choice, as shown at the top of the opposite page.

Single-click the disclosure triangle to display the rest of the dialog box.

To hide the extra information, single-click this triangle again.

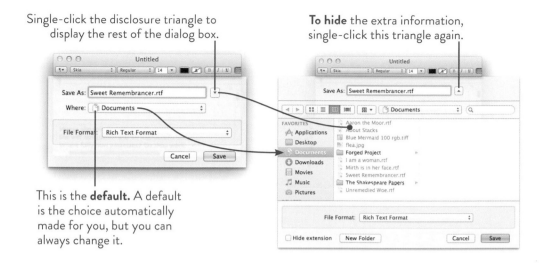

This is the **default.** A default is the choice automatically made for you, but you can always change it.

You will regularly see little **color wells** (shown circled, below left and center) in places where you can choose to change the colors of things. Whenever you see one, simply single-click it to make the "Colors" palette appear.

Color wells

This is the View Options for a Finder window. You can change the background color of the window.

In the application called Keynote, click the color well to change the color of **selected** text.

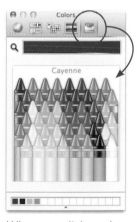

When you click a color well, this Colors palette appears. Above, the crayon box icon in the toolbar is chosen. You can choose another icon in the toolbar for different options for choosing colors.

Remember...

- Before you choose something from a menu, make sure you **select the item** to which you want the command to apply.

  For instance, if you want to close a window, first single-click the window you want to close. If you want to make a duplicate of something, first single-click the item you want to duplicate.

- Take advantage of the **keyboard shortcuts.** Check the menu to first find out what the shortcut is, then later use that shortcut *instead* of going to the menu.

- Did you notice in the contextual menus on page 57 that there is an option called **Label** with colored dots? You can choose one of those colors, and it will make the selected icon that color. This can be a handy organizing tool—color all your love letters red, all tax files mustard, all research papers blue, etc. Later, you can search for files of a particular color of label (see pages 174–177 about searching).

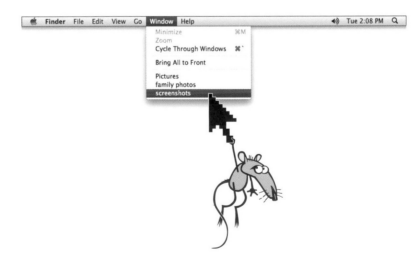

Use an
Application 6

This chapter covers what you will do most often on your Mac: **open an application** and **type a document.** Do the exercises, and then in the following chapter, you'll save the document you create, print it, close it, and quit the application.

You're going to use the TextEdit application in this chapter, but the process will apply to any application you ever use: First, you have to open the application. Then you open a document *within* that application. You do some sort of work on it. You'll save it, most of the time you will print it, then quit. So don't go through the exercises in these two chapters as if you are learning how to use TextEdit—you are really learning the process of creating new documents on your Macintosh. *Each exercise assumes you followed the previous exercise.*

Almost everything you learn in this chapter will also apply to writing email, so be sure not to skip this!

In this chapter

Open an application. 64	Alignment 75
Open a blank document 65	Cut, Copy, and the Clipboard 76
New vs. Open. 65	Cut. 77
I-beam. 66	Copy. 78
Insertion point 66	Paste. 79
Delete (or Backspace) 68	Undo 81
Delete characters. 68	Keyboard shortcuts 82
Spell checking. 69	Delete or Clear and the Clipboard. . . .82
Control spell checking. 70	Access special characters 82
One space after periods 71	Use real accent marks 83
Select (highlight) text 72	Document windows 84
Replace highlighted text. 73	**Also Try This**. 85
Extra tips. 73	**Remember**. 86
Change fonts and type size. 74	

Open an application

An **application** is a program in which you do things, like write letters, design flyers or artwork, organize and edit your photos, make movies, send email, etc. Different applications have different purposes. In this chapter, you're going to open and work in a **word processor,** which is a program specifically meant for typing. Other applications are for creating databases or spreadsheets, or for painting, drawing, or building web pages, etc. In Chapter 10, you'll use an application called a **browser** that is specifically for viewing web pages.

The word processor you'll use in this chapter is called TextEdit and it came with your Mac. If you did the exercises in Chapter 3 (page 32, specifically), TextEdit is now in your Dock, so follow Exercise 1a; if not, do Exercise 1b, below.

TextEdit

Exercise 1a: Open TextEdit if its icon is in your Dock. (If not, skip to Exercise 1b.)

1 Locate the TextEdit icon in your Dock.

2 Single-click the icon.

OR . . .

Exercise 1b: Open TextEdit if its icon is not in your Dock.

Launchpad

1 Find the Launchpad icon in your Dock; single-click it.

2 Find the TextEdit icon on the screen (they're in alphabetical order); single-click it.

If Launchpad is not in your Dock, open a Finder window (single-click the Finder icon in the Dock). In the Sidebar, single-click "Applications." Find TextEdit (you can type the letters TE to find and select it), then double-click its icon.

TextEdit automatically opens a **blank document window,** ready for you to work.

> You will, at some point, open an application that doesn't automatically provide a blank window. In that case, just go to the File menu and choose "New."
>
> At some point you might also want to choose a new blank window when you've finished with one document and want to get started on another. You don't have to quit the application—just open a "New" document. You can have as many documents open at once as you like.

Open a blank document

The first time I went to the File menu to open a blank document, I saw the options **New** and **Open.** And I thought, "Well, I want to OPEN a NEW one." It confused me mightily. This is the difference:

New vs. Open

> NEW: Opens a blank, untitled, unsaved document.
>
> OPEN: Opens a dialog box where you can choose an existing document of your choice that has already been titled and saved. Perhaps you want to continue working on it or make changes (see page 89).

Exercise 2: Type.

1. One quick thing before you start typing: Go to the "Format" menu in TextEdit and look for the command "Wrap to Page." If you find it, choose it (if it says "Wrap to Window," that means what you see is already "Wrap to Page"; skip to Step 2). The "Wrap to Page" option displays your page closer to what it will look like when you print it.

This is called "Wrap to Window."

2. Just start typing. Type at least a paragraph, *ignoring typos for now.*

   At the ends of lines, **do not** hit the Return key—the text, as you type, will bump into the far-right edge and bounce back to the left side automatically.

3. **Do** hit the Return key at the end of a paragraph. Hit it twice if you want a double space between your paragraphs.

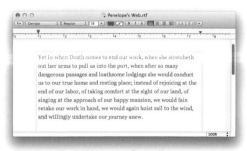

This is called "Wrap to Page."

4. Go to the next page in this book and read about the **insertion point** and the **I-beam,** then continue with the exercises.

I-beam

You may already be familiar with the Macintosh word processing **I-beam** (pronounced *eye-beam*). It looks like this: ⌶

The tiny crossbar just below the center of the I-beam indicates the "baseline" of type, the invisible line that type sits upon.

On the Mac, the I-beam is a **visual clue** that you are now in a typing mode, as opposed to seeing an arrow or a crosshair or any number of other "cursors" that appear in various applications.

- *The I-beam is simply another pointer.* And just like the pointer, it doesn't do anything until you click it or press-and-drag it.

Insertion point

When you move the I-beam pointer to a spot within text and *single-click,* it sets down a flashing **insertion point** that looks like this: | (but it flashes).

This insertion point is extremely important! First you click the mouse to *set* the insertion point, then you *move the I-beam* out of the way (using the mouse)—**the insertion point is what you need to begin typing,** not the I-beam!!

The I-beam merely positions the insertion point.

Note: The only time the words will not move to the right in a word processor is if the text is centered or flush right, as described on page 75, or if you've set a tab other than left-aligned.

With the insertion point flashing, anything you type will start at that point and move out to the right. This is true whether the insertion point is at the beginning or the end of a paragraph, in the middle of a word, in a field of a dialog box, in the name of an icon at your Desktop, or anywhere else.

If you noticed, when you first opened a new, blank document in TextEdit, there was an insertion point flashing in the upper-left corner, indicating you could start typing immediately.

To begin typing somewhere else at any time, you can use the mouse/trackpad to move the I-beam pointer anywhere in the existing text, click to set the insertion point, move the I-beam out of the way, and start typing from the new insertion point.

To type below the existing text, set the insertion point directly after the last character in the text, then hit the Return key a number of times until the insertion point is where you want to begin typing.

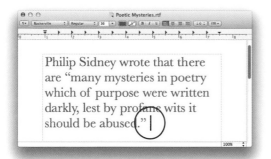 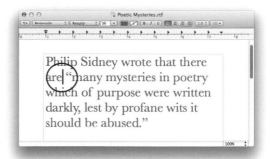

Do you see the insertion point at the end of the paragraph? If I start to type again in this story, the typing will begin at that insertion point.

The I-beam (do you see it?) is just hanging around waiting to be useful.

Do you see where I moved the insertion point to? If I start to type again in this story, the new text will begin at that insertion point.

Do you see the I-beam?

Exercise 3: Learn to be conscious of the I-beam and the insertion point.

1 Type a few more letters on your page. Notice how the **insertion point** constantly stays ahead of the characters as you type.

2 Stop typing. Move the mouse around or drag your finger around the trackpad, and notice that the cursor is not a pointer, but an **I-beam.**

(The cursor becomes a pointer when you move off of the word processing page, but when you position it over the text, it becomes the I-beam.)

3 Using your mouse or trackpad:
   • Position that I-beam anywhere in your paragraph,
      . . . single-click,
      . . . shove the mouse (and thus the I-beam) out of the way,
      . . . and start typing.

   Notice the insertion point moves to where you click the I-beam, and your new typing starts at that point.

4 Single-click the I-beam at the very end of the existing text—this will set the insertion point there. Now it's ready for you to continue typing at the end of your story.

Delete
(or Backspace)

When you press the **Delete** key (found in the upper right of the main part of the keyboard), it deletes anything **to the *left* of the insertion point.**

You can backspace/delete to **correct typos** (typographical errors) as you type, *or* you can click to set the insertion point down anywhere else in your text and backspace from that new position.

After you make a correction and you want to continue typing at the end of your story, single-click the I-beam at the end of the story to set the insertion point there, then type.

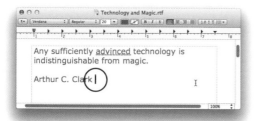

This paragraph has a typo in the first line. Do you see it? TextEdit has underlined the typo with red dots. I need to fix it.

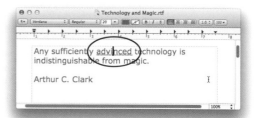

I used the I-beam to set the insertion point just to the **right** of the typo. Now I can hit the Delete key to erase that wrong letter and type the correct one in its place.

Delete characters

Exercise 4: Edit your text.

1 In the text on your page, notice where the insertion point is flashing.

2 Hit the **Delete** key several times. Watch as it deletes the characters **to the left** of the insertion point.

3 Now, using your mouse:
   • Position that I-beam anywhere in your paragraph,
      . . . single-click,
      . . . shove the mouse (and I-beam) out of the way,
      . . . and hit the Delete key one or more times.

   Notice TextEdit deletes text to the left of the insertion point. Every Mac program will do the same thing.

4 Using the mouse, position the I-beam **at the end** of your text.

5 Click to set the insertion point (then move the mouse/I-beam out of the way) so you can start typing again from the end of your document.

Spell checking

You've probably noticed that TextEdit puts **red dots** under words that it thinks are **misspelled.** If the word is *not* misspelled, you can just ignore the red dots—they won't print. But if you want to fix a typo, here's a great trick (and it works in Mail, too):

Exercise 5: Experiment with spell checking.

1 Hold down the Command key and single-click anywhere in the misspelled word. This makes a contextual menu pop up, like the ones you used in Chapter 5.

2 TextEdit provides a list of possible words, based on the misspelled word. If you see the correct spelling, single-click it and the typo is corrected; if you don't see the correct spelling, click anywhere on the page to get rid of the menu, then make the correction yourself.

If you don't see a list of possible words, it means the word is spelled correctly or not in the dictionary.

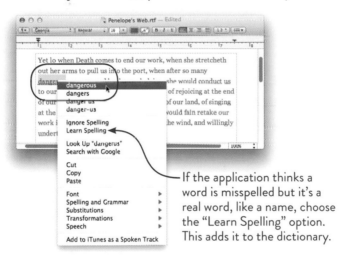

If the application thinks a word is misspelled but it's a real word, like a name, choose the "Learn Spelling" option. This adds it to the dictionary.

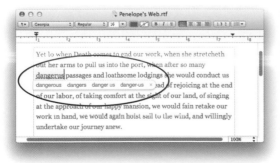

Sometimes TextEdit offers you possible options for misspelled words, as shown to the left. When you see these, either click on the word you want, *or* click the tiny **x** at the end of the row to delete the options, or hit the Spacebar to accept the first word in the list.

To control the spelling options, see the next page.

Control spell checking   As you've been typing, you surely noticed that TextEdit attempts to correct your spelling along the way, and even automatically changes the spelling sometimes. This auto-correction can create some pretty funny (or horrifying) messages, if you're not careful.

You can change the preferences any time you like so TextEdit does what *you* want it to do. It's good to know how to control this so it won't make you crazy.

Exercise 6a: Check out the spell checking options.

1 Go to the Edit menu and slide down to "Spelling and Grammar."

2 In the submenu, a checkmark next to "Check Spelling While Typing" means it *will* check your spelling.

   To tell it to *stop* checking your spelling, choose that item again to *uncheck* the command.

3 In that same menu, there might be a checkmark next to "Correct Spelling Automatically."

   To turn auto-correct off, choose that command, which will remove the checkmark. (I know, it seems a bit odd at first to choose a command to turn it off, but many commands have these checkmark "toggle" switches.)

   That is, choose the command to either put a checkmark there *or* to remove the existing checkmark, depending on what you want it to do.

Exercise 6b: Change the preferences for future documents.

Now, this will turn off these features for this open document. To change the settings for all future TextEdit documents you open:

1 Go to the TextEdit menu and choose "Preferences...."

2 Make sure the "New Document" tab is chosen (single-click on it).

3 At the bottom of the pane are a number of "Options" for spelling and grammar corrections. Make your choices.

4 To put the preferences away, single-click the red close button in the upper-left of the pane. Now all future documents you create will have these settings.

What?! **One space after a period?** If you grew up on a typewriter, this is a difficult habit to change, I know. Or if you were taught keyboarding skills by someone who grew up on a typewriter, they taught you typewriter rules. But characters on a Mac are not *monospaced* as they are on a typewriter (except for a few typefaces such as Monaco, Courier, and Andale Mono), so there is no need to use two spaces to separate two sentences. Check any book or magazine on your shelf; you will never find two spaces after periods (except publications produced on a computer typed by someone still using typewriter rules).

If you find this hard to accept, read *The Mac is not a typewriter.* It's a very little book. If you're interested in creating fine typography, read *The Non-Designer's Type Book.* Yes, I wrote them.

For the ultimate authority, check the question-and-answer page on the web site for the *Chicago Manual of Style:*

www.ChicagoManualofStyle.org

One space after periods

See Chapter 10 for details on how to go to a web page.

You can skip this for now, but at some point return here to learn how to increase the space between the lines to give the text more breathing room and thus make it easier to read. TextEdit has made this very easy for you!

Adjust the linespacing

Extra Credit: Adjust the linespacing.

1 Select everything you've typed in the document: Press Command A to "Select All."

2 In the Toolbar, click the *Line and paragraph spacing* button, as shown below.

3 Choose 1.2 or 1.3 and notice how much nicer it looks!

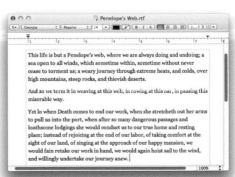

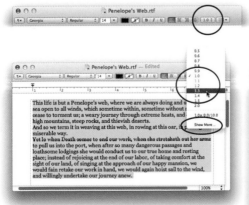

Notice how much easier it is to read text with a little extra linespace. I also added 8 points of "Paragraph spacing, after"—choose "Show More..." if you want to do that.

Select (highlight) text

When you **select text,** it becomes **highlighted.** Once text is selected, you can do things to it, such as change its size, the typeface, delete it, etc.

If you use the I-beam to double-click a word anywhere on the Mac, the entire word is selected, indicated by the highlighting.

This `word` is highlighted. I double-clicked the word to select it.

To select more than one word, *press-and-drag* over the entire area you wish to highlight. `This entire sentence is highlighted.`

To select all of the text in an entire document, use the keyboard shortcut Command A.

Exercise 7: **Experiment with selecting text.**

1 In the paragraph you typed earlier, position the I-beam in the middle of any word.

2 **Double-click** the word to select it. Try it on different words until you feel comfortable selecting whole words.

3 **Now select a range of text:**

   • Position the I-beam somewhere toward the top of a paragraph,

      . . . press the mouse/trackpad button down and hold it down,

      . . . then drag the cursor downward. (You can move up as well, or straight left or right, as long as you keep the button down.)

   • When you have a range of text selected, let go of the mouse/trackpad button.

   • Try it several times until you feel comfortable selecting a range of text.

To un-highlight (deselect) text, single-click anywhere, even in the highlighted space.

Once a word is selected (highlighted), anything you type will **entirely replace the selected text.** That is, you don't have to hit the Delete key first to get rid of the text—just type. This is true everywhere on the Mac.

Replace highlighted text

Exercise 8: *Delete* selected text, and also *replace* selected text with new text.

1 In the paragraph you typed earlier, use the I-beam to double-click a word to select it.

2 Hit the **Delete** key once to delete the selected word. Do this several times until it feels very comfortable.

3 Now, double-click a word to select it, *or* press-and-drag to select a range of text.

4 *Do not* hit the Delete key this time: Just type a new word and watch it **replace** the selected text.

5 Try selecting a range of text and while it is highlighted, type a new sentence. Repeat until it feels comfortable.

Try these tips for **moving the insertion point** and for **selecting text** anywhere on the Mac:

Extra tips

- Use the arrow keys to move the insertion point backward and forward, up and down.

- Hold down the Shift key as you hit the arrow keys, and the text will be *selected* along the way. Try it.

- Triple-click in the middle of a sentence to select the entire paragraph. (In some applications, a triple-click will select one single line instead of the entire paragraph).

- This is my favorite selection trick:
  - **Single-click** at the point where you want to begin the selection; the insertion point will flash,
    - . . . move the I-beam to where you want the selection to end (don't drag with the mouse button down and don't click anything yet!),
    - . . . hold down the **Shift** key,
    - . . . **Single-click** where you want the selection to end.

  I call this the *Click Shift-Click* Trick.

Change fonts (typefaces) and type size

Throughout the entire Mac environment, to make any changes to anything you must follow *Rule Number Two:*

Select First, Then Do It to It.

For instance, **to change text to a different font,** or typeface:

1 First you'll *select* the characters you want to change.

2 Then you'll *choose* the font that you want to apply to the text.

Exercise 9: Add a headline to your text, and then change the headline font, size, and color.

1 First **add a headline** at the beginning of the paragraph you typed earlier. To do that:

> With the mouse, move the I-beam to the beginning of the text; position it to the *left* of the very first letter.
>
> Single-click at that position to set the insertion point. If you miss and the insertion point is a letter or two to the right or perhaps on the next line down, use the arrow keys to move the insertion point to the very beginning of the first line.

2 Type a headline of some sort, something like *My Important Headline.* The existing text will move along to the right as you type the new headline.

3 At the end of your headline, hit Return twice.

4 Now **select the headline:** Starting at one end or the other of the headline, press-and-drag over the text so you select every character (*or* triple-click in the line.)

5 In the Toolbar, single-click on the *font family* button, and choose a font.

> Single-click the *typeface* button to choose a style.
>
> Single-click the *font size* button and choose a point size, *or* type a number into the tiny field.
>
> Single-click the color "well" and choose a color. Voilà!

Use the formatting tools in the Toolbar to format the *selected* text.

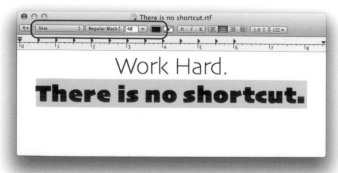

Alignment refers to where the text is lined up.

Alignment

Align left: Text is lined up on the
left side, and the right is "ragged,"
as shown in these short lines.

Align right: Text is lined up
on the right, and
the left edge is ragged.
This is also known as flush right.

Align center:
Text is centered on a vertical axis
between your margins.
If you change your margins,
your centered text
will shift.

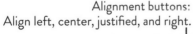

Justified: Text is lined up on both
the left and right margins, as you
can see in this short little paragraph.

To change your alignment, you know what to do! That's right:
Select first, then do it to it—highlight the text, then choose the
alignment from the Toolbar buttons, as shown below, or from
the menu commands (under the "Format" menu, choose "Text"
and you'll see the alignment options).

Alignment buttons:
Align left, center, justified, and right.

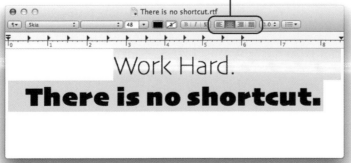

In this example, you can see that the text is selected
(highlighted) and the center alignment button is checked.

TIP: When you plan to
change the alignment,
you don't have to select
every character in the line
or paragraph—to select
an entire paragraph, just
single-click in it. The
paragraph will not be
highlighted, but it will
be **selected.** Try it.

Cut, Copy, and the Clipboard

Almost anywhere you can type, you can cut or copy text.

When you **cut** text (or a graphic), it is **removed** from your document and placed on the "Clipboard."

When you **copy** text (or a graphic), the original text is **intact** in your document and a *copy* of it is placed on the Clipboard.

Well, what the heck is a Clipboard?

The **Clipboard** is an invisible "container" somewhere in the depths of the Mac. It temporarily holds whatever you have cut or copied, be it text, spreadsheet data, graphics, an entire folder, etc. Once something is on the Clipboard, it waits there until you **paste** it somewhere (we'll get to that in a minute).

The most important thing to remember about the Clipboard is that *it holds only one thing at a time;* that is, as soon as you cut or copy something else, whatever was in the Clipboard is replaced by the new selection.

In some programs, including the Finder, you'll find a menu command called "Show Clipboard," usually in the Edit menu. When you can see it, the Clipboard appears as a window with its contents displayed, as shown below. In most programs, though, you never see the actual Clipboard—you have to simply trust it.

The Clipboard appears as a window (if it's available for looking at in your program). You can always go to the Finder, open the Edit menu, and choose "Show Clipboard" to see what you've got.

Items will stay on the Clipboard even when you change applications. For instance, you can put a paint image on the Clipboard in a paint program, then open a word processing document and paste the paint image into a letter.

Items disappear from the Clipboard when the computer is turned off or if there is a power failure, so don't count on keeping something in the Clipboard for very long!

How to Cut: Select first, then do it to it. Remember, whatever you cut will *disappear* from the document.   **Cut**

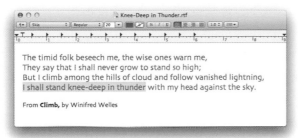

The text is selected and ready to be cut.

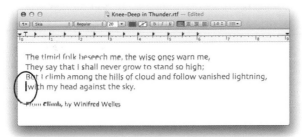

The text has been cut. All that's left is the insertion point.

Exercise 10: Cut some text.

1 Select the text you wish to remove from the document (press-and-drag over the text).

2 From the Edit menu, choose "Cut."

The text will be *eliminated* from your document and placed on the Clipboard. Now you can paste it somewhere; see the following pages.

Be sure to read about the differences between "Cut" and "Clear" or "Delete" on page 82.

To undo the cut you just made, go to the Edit menu and choose "Undo Cut."

Copy

How to Copy: Select first, then do it to it.

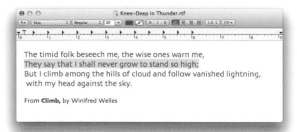

This text is selected, ready to be copied.

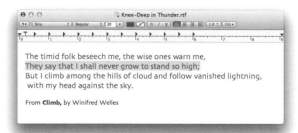

The text has been copied, and it looks like
nothing happened because the text is still there.
That's exactly what is supposed to happen.

So the copied text is on the Clipboard. Now what? Well, the Clipboard holds objects for *pasting*. You can take text or a graphic out
of one place and paste it into your document somewhere else, just
as if you had a little glue pot. We'll get to that in just a moment
(next page).

Exercise 11: Copy some text.

1 Select the text you wish to copy.

2 From the Edit menu, choose "Copy."

The text *remains* in your document and a *copy* is
placed on the Clipboard. Now you can paste it in
the next exercise.

Paste

How to Paste: When you go to the Edit menu and choose "Paste," you need to tell your Mac *where* to paste it.

- Whatever was on the Clipboard will be inserted in your document *beginning at the flashing insertion point.* So if you want the pasted item to appear at a certain place in your document, **first** click the I-beam to position the insertion point.

- If you have a *range of text selected,* the pasted item will **replace** what was selected.

As long as something is on the Clipboard, you can paste it anywhere else a million times in many different applications.

In other types of applications, like drawing and painting applications, a pasted object will usually just land in the middle of the page.

Exercise 12: Paste some text.

1 Because you previously cut or copied some text, you know there is text on the Clipboard waiting to be pasted. (If you didn't do Exercise 8 or 9, do one of them now so you have something on the Clipboard.)

2 *Position the I-beam* where you want to paste in the text, then *click* to set the insertion point.

3 Go to the Edit menu and choose "Paste." The text will be pasted in beginning at that insertion point.

And then:

4 Repeat Steps 2 and 3 (above) several more times. Notice you can keep pasting in the same text over and over.

5 Cut or copy some *other* text, then repeat Steps 2 and 3 above. Notice you are now pasting the *other* text.

On the following page is an example of each step in the cut-and-paste process.

Exercise 13: Cut a paragraph and paste it somewhere else.

1 Type several paragraphs on your page, if you haven't already.

2 Change the formatting of the first paragraph so it looks very different: Change the font, the typeface style, and the size.

3 Triple-click anywhere in the formatted paragraph to select the entire paragraph.

4 Use the keyboard shortcut to cut the selected paragraph: Command X.

5 Set the insertion point at the end of your text and hit two Returns.

6 Press Command V (the keyboard shortcut) to paste the paragraph in, starting at the insertion point.

79

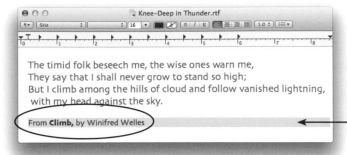

An example of the cut-and-paste process

I triple-clicked the by-line to select the entire "paragraph." Remember, every time you hit the Return key, the Mac thinks you have made another paragraph.

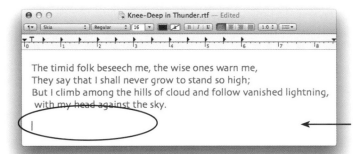

I **cut** the selected text. Now it's on the Clipboard, waiting for me to paste it somewhere.

Using the I-beam, I clicked right before the first word in the paragraph to set the insertion point (circled). When I paste, the text will be inserted at that insertion point.

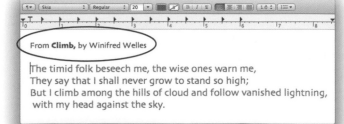

Here is the text, after pasting it in. You might need to hit a Return or two after you paste so you have space after the line.

Exercise 14: Copy a heading from one document and paste it into another document.

1   On the page you've been working with, type something like a headline. Format it (choose a font, typeface style, and size).

2   Select the text you just formatted.

3   Either cut or copy the selected text.

4   Open a new TextEdit window: Go to the File menu and choose "New," *or* use the keyboard shortcut Command N.

5   In the new window (which is a new document), type a few lines.

6   Set the insertion point and paste—the headline you formatted and copied from the other document is now in this new document.

Undo can sometimes save your boompah (no, that's not computer jargon—it's Grandma's euphemism).

Undo

When you do something that makes you scream, "Aack! Oh no!" try Undo. It's always the first command in the Edit menu (or press Command Z).

Important Note: What Undo can undo is *only the last action that occurred*. For instance, if you selected two paragraphs of brilliantly witty text that you spent three hours composing and then the cat walked across your keyboard and obliterated the entire work, Undo could give it back to you **IF** you Undo before you touch *anything*. Don't start fiddling around with the keys and the mouse because then what you will undo is that fiddling around.

So if something goes wrong, don't scream—**UNDO.**

Then scream.

(Some applications, such as illustration programs and page layout applications, can Undo multiple steps. Check your manual.)

Keyboard shortcuts

In Chapter 5 you learned how to use keyboard shortcuts for various tasks. Thoughtfully, the **keyboard shortcuts** for the Undo, Cut, Copy, and Paste commands are very handy. Notice on your keyboard the letters **Z, X, C,** and **V,** all lined up in a row right above the Command key—these are the shortcut keys.

Remember, select first (*except to Undo*); then hold down the Command key and lightly tap the letter.

Command **Z** will Undo	Z is very close to the Command key.
Command **X** will Cut	X like Xing it out.
Command **C** will Copy	C for Copy.
Command **V** will Paste	V because it is next to C; it's sort of like the caret symbol ^ for inserting.

Delete or Clear and the Clipboard

Now, the **Delete** key (on the upper right of the main group of keys) works a little differently from the Cut command:

Delete: If you hit the Delete key while something is selected, whatever is selected is *deleted* but is *not* placed on the Clipboard.

This means if you are holding something in the Clipboard to paste in again, whatever you delete from your document will *not* replace what you are currently holding in the Clipboard.

But it also means that you don't have that deleted item anymore—*whatever you delete is really gone and cannot be pasted anywhere* (but remember, you can Undo!).

Clear, in the Edit menu, is the same as Delete.

Access special characters

Special characters are the symbols you have access to on your Mac that weren't available on typewriters, such as upside-down question marks for Spanish (¿), the pound symbol for English money (£), the cents sign (¢), the registration or trademark symbols (® ™), the copyright symbol (©), etc.

Following is a short list of special characters you can experiment with. For each character, hold down the modifier key (Option, Shift, etc.) and tap the character key noted. For instance, to type a bullet, hold down the Option key and tap the number 8 on the top of your keyboard (not the number 8 on the keypad). It's no different from typing an asterisk, where you hold down the Shift key and tap the 8.

·	*bullet*	Option	8
©	*copyright*	Option	G
¢	*cents*	Option	$
€	*euro*	Option Shift	2

A complete list of special characters is on page 201.

You can type **accent marks** on the Mac, as in résumé or piñata. In most apps from Apple, such as TextEdit and Pages, you can use the first technique explained in Exercise 15a.

Use real accent marks

Exercise 15a: Type the word résumé:

1 Type the word until you come to the letter that will be *under* the accent mark; e.g., **e**.

2 Now, instead of typing an e, *hold down* the e key until you see accent options appear.

3 Tap the number of the character you want.

If your application doesn't supply the accent marks as shown above, they're easy to insert using the Option key. The marks hide beneath the keyboard characters that would usually be under them. For example, the acute accent over the **é** is **Option e**; the tilde over the **ñ** is **Option n.**

Here is a list of common accent marks:

´	Option e
`	Option ~
¨	Option u
~	Option n
^	Option i

A complete list is on pages 202–203.

Exercise 15b: Type the word résumé:

1 Type the word until you come to the letter that will be *under* the accent mark; e.g., **e**.

2 *Before* you type that next letter (the letter **e** in this case), type the Option combination (**Option e** in this case, which means hold down the Option key and tap the **e** once)—*it will look like nothing happened, or you might see the accent mark and a highlight.* That's okay.

3 Now let go of the Option key. Type the character that is to be *under* the accent mark. Both the mark and the letter will appear together; e.g., **r é**.

4 Type the rest of the word: **r é s u m é**.

Now try typing *Voilà!*

83

Document windows

Document windows are very similar to Finder windows, but they do have a few differences.

You can tell the window below is a **document window** because in the menu bar across the top of the monitor, just to the right of the apple, is the name of the application in which this document is open. This is the Preview application, which is on your Mac (if it's not in your Dock, find it in Launchpad); when you double-click a photograph, it usually opens automatically in Preview.

Document windows sometimes have Sidebars, and they usually have their own Toolbars with buttons and options appropriate to the specific application.

This is the name of the application whose window is active.

This is the name, or **title,** of the document that is open in this application.

Each document you create will be in its own window.

Just like any Finder window, you can **resize** a document window (drag any corner or edge), **move** it (drag the title bar), **scroll** through it (drag a scroll bar or use swiping gestures), and **close** it (click in the red button). Check it out.

Also Try This

Double-Return: Hitting the Return key twice creates a double space between the lines. This is for extra space between individual paragraphs.

If you want the **entire document,** or even just a piece of it, **double-spaced,** it can be easier to do this: In TextEdit, select all (press Command A) *or* select the paragraphs you want double-spaced. Single-click the "Spacing" button in the Toolbar, then choose "2.0."

Remove a Return: The computer sees a Return as just another character, which means to *remove* a Return you simply backspace over it with the Delete key, just as you would to remove an unwanted character. The problem is that in most programs you can't *see* the Return character. Just set the insertion point to the *left* of the first character on the line, then Delete, as shown:

> Let's say I'm typing away and my dog shoves her big head under my arm and suddenly
>
> my text starts typing on the wrong line, like this. What to do?

Set the insertion point directly to the *left* of the text that's on the wrong line (as shown below).

> Let's say I'm typing away and my dog shoves her big head under my arm and suddenly
>
> my text starts typing on the wrong line, like this. What to do?

Hit the Delete key to remove the empty line above that new, unwanted paragraph (*you* don't think it's a paragraph, but the computer does). Now it looks like this:

> Let's say I'm typing away and my dog shoves her big head under my arm and suddenly
> my text starts typing on the wrong line, like this. What to do?

Delete again to wrap the sentence back up to the one above.

> Let's say I'm typing away and my dog shoves her big head under my arm and suddenly my text starts typing on the wrong line, like this. What to do? Oh, it's all fixed!

Move the insertion point back to where you want to begin typing.

Remember....

- Use the **I-beam** only to move and set the **insertion point.** The insertion point is the important thing—that's where type will start typing, and that's where text or graphics will paste in.

- Only type **one space after periods** or any other punctuation.

- Cut, Copy, Paste, Undo, Clear, and Delete are the same all over the Mac, everywhere you go. The **keyboard shortcuts** are always the same.

Save & Print 7

You must **save your document** if you ever want to see it again; that is, you'll save an electronic file in your computer. And of course you must **print it** if you want to see your work on paper, which is really the only way to save something permanently.

This chapter uses the document you created in Chapter 6. If you haven't done those exercises yet, take a moment now to open a new TextEdit document and type several paragraphs so you can work with the exercises and experiments in this chapter.

In this chapter

Save your document 88
Save regularly 90
    Explore the saved versions 90
Duplicate a document 91
    Duplicate a document the Apple way . . . 91
    Duplicate a document another way 92
Print your document 93
Add a printer to the list, if necessary 94
Page setup 96
Print specifications 97
    Application-specific options 97
    See a preview 98
    Copies & Pages 99
    Layout 100
    Print-specific options 101
Using the print queue window 102
    Control your print jobs 102
    Keep your printer icon in the Dock . . . 105
Remember 106

Save your document

If you are new to computers, all you need to do is this **quick-and-easy save.** This will store your document in the Documents folder, which is accessible from the Sidebar in every Finder window.

You don't have to wait until your document is finished before you save it. In fact, you should save and title it as soon as you start, and then keep saving the changes along the way, explained below.

Even though Lion will automatically save your file for you every hour and also when you close the document, if you haven't *titled* the document, it cannot be automatically saved. If something happens like the power goes out for a split second, you have lost forever whatever was not saved! Remember *Rule Number One:* **SOS** (Save Often, Sweetie!).

Exercise 1: Save your document with a name, or title.

TIP: Give your document a title you will remember! A title like "Memo" is going to confuse you when you have a folder full of thirty memos.

1 Make sure the document you want to save is open, in front of you, and *active*—single-click it to make sure.

2 From the File menu, choose "Save…." This opens the "Save As" dialog box, shown below.

3 Type the name of your file in the "Save As" field, as pointed out below.

Type the name of your document here.

This tells you the folder in which your document will be stored.

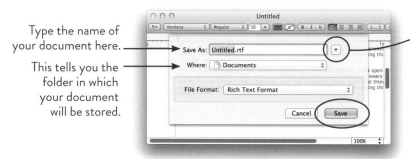

4 Click the Save button (or hit the Return or Enter key).

You're all done! The Mac has saved your file into the Documents folder, as shown on the opposite page. Your document appears in front of you again so you can continue working on it.

 From now on, press Command S **every few minutes** to **update** the new changes you've made as you work (you won't see a dialog box when you press Command S). This ensures that if something happens, you won't lose more than a couple of minutes of work.

If you want, you can skip to the printing part of this chapter now! (See page 93.)

If you want **to save your document into a different folder** than the one that is automatically offered to you, simply click the disclosure triangle (circled on the opposite page) to get more options, as shown below.

Click this disclosure triangle to show or hide the rest of the dialog box, as you can see here.

This window shows you exactly where your file is going to be stored—you can see that this file will go into the Documents folder.

If you know you need a different file format (for instance, you need to send a Word document to someone), click this menu and choose another format.

Once you have titled and saved a document, its icon appears in the folder in which you saved it, as shown below.

To open that document again, double-click its icon.

Save regularly Apple applications (and some third-party ones) provide a **visual clue** if your document has unsaved changes: Next to the title you will see "Edited." Just press **Command S** to **save** the changes; use this keyboard shortcut regularly, like every couple of minutes.

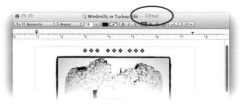

This reminder indicates you need to save the changes you've made to the document: Command S.

Explore the saved versions Every time you save a document in an Apple application (and those that follow the Apple guidelines), your Mac creates a new **version** for you, and even if you completely forget, the Mac will automatically save a version every hour. At any point you can look at these versions and go back to a previous one, if you like.

Exercise 2: View previous versions of your document.

1 Create a document in TextEdit. Save it with a name (see page 88), then continue working on the document. Notice the "Edited" reminder in the title bar. Save regularly using Command S.

2 Position your pointer over the title; a tiny triangle will appear. *Press* on the title to get the menu shown below; choose "Browse All Versions...."

You will see the "versions" view of your document, as shown on the opposite page, with a separate file for every time it was saved.

Click on a document title bar to see that version, scroll through the document, choose a date or time from the timeline on the right side of the screen, or choose to

"Restore" a selected version (the one that is visible on the right is the one that will be restored).

Click "Done" to return to TextEdit if you don't want to restore anything.

Duplicate a document

Sometimes you might want to create changes in a document, but you still want to keep a **copy of the original without the changes.** For instance, let's say you write a witty letter to Uncle Jerry, then decide you also want to write to Uncle Floyd. You have a few things to tell Floyd that Jerry isn't interested in, but you don't want to retype the entire letter.

How to accomplish this task depends on whether you are using an Apple application (see below) or an application that you installed from another vendor (see the following page).

Exercise 3a: Make a duplicate.

Duplicate a document the Apple way

1 Create a document in TextEdit. When it is complete and saved, *press* on the title bar to get the menu shown below.

2 Choose "Duplicate." A new document appears.

3 Press Command S and save it with a different name.

The duplicate document lands on top of the original. Be sure to give it a new name.

Duplicate a document another way If the document you're working on does not remind you that it has been "edited" in the title bar, it probably doesn't have the little menu with the option to "Duplicate." No problem. This is when you'll use "Save As…" *a second time* to give the document *a new name,* which actually creates a new, separate file and leaves the original file intact.

Exercise 3b: Make another version based on the original.

1 Create a new document (go to the File menu and choose "New," *or* press Command N). Type a few witty paragraphs in this new document.

2 Save this original document and give it a name (as explained on page 88). Let's say you've named it "Witty letter to Uncle Jerry." *Don't close the document.*

3 While that document is still open on the screen, from the File menu, choose "Save As…" *again.*

4 Change the name, say from "Witty letter to Uncle Jerry" to "Witty letter to Uncle Floyd."

This automatically puts the *original* document (to Uncle Jerry) safely away on your disk and *creates a new one* (the copy to Uncle Floyd) right on the screen. You'll notice the name in the title bar of your document changes to what you renamed it. *Any changes you make to this new document (Uncle Floyd's) will not affect the original, Uncle Jerry's.*

Jerry's
garden.pages

Jeffrey's
garden.pages

Floyd's
garden.pages

Merv's
garden.pages

All of these garden newsletters are based on the original for Uncle Jerry. I just kept choosing "Save As" and giving the new ones new names.

The information, layout, type choices, etc., all stayed the same, but now each newsletter is separate and I can add or delete details in each.

Print your document

On this page are the briefest of directions for **printing your pages.** If it works, then you can skip the rest of this chapter, unless you want to understand what some of the options are. For this very quick start, make sure the printer is plugged into the wall *and* into the computer with the appropriate cables; there is paper in the printer; and the printer is turned on and warmed up (wait until it stops making noises). Then:

Exercise 4: Print your document.

1 Open the document that you want to print.

2 From the File menu, choose "Print...."

3 Click the "Print" button (or hit the Return key).

That's all. **If it worked,** skip to page 96 if you want to learn about some of the printing options.

If the "Printer" menu in the dialog box, circled below, says **"No Printer Selected,"** go to the next page and follow the directions to add your printer to the list. You only have to do this once and then printing will be as easy as the three steps above.

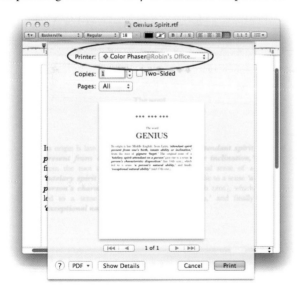

This is typically what you will see when you choose to Print. There are lots of settings that you won't see until you click the blue disclosure triangle, as explained on the following pages. But if you just want to print the pages in your document to make sure printing works, you can safely hit the "Print" button without bothering about anything else.

TIP: Do you see the button **"PDF ▼"**? If you click that and choose "Save as PDF...," your Mac makes a PDF file of this document for you, which is a special type of file that you can send to anyone on any kind of computer, and it will look just like it does on your Mac.

Add a printer to the list, if necessary

Your Mac needs to put your printer in its "Printer List" so you can choose to print to it and so the computer knows what that particular printer is capable of doing. For instance, if you print to an inexpensive color inkjet, the Print dialog box will provide color options, but probably not paper tray options; if you print to a color PostScript laser printer, you might have double-sided page options or larger paper sizes.

The more expensive the printer, the more important it is to first install the software that came with it! So take a few moments to do that, if necessary.

To add a printer to the Printer List, you can either use the Print dialog box in your document (5a), **or** the Print & Scan system preferences (5b). Either method has the same result, as follows:

Exercise 5a: Use the Print dialog box to add a printer.

1   Turn on the printer that you want to add to the list. Wait until it is fully warmed up (wait until it stops making noise and the green light is not flashing).

2   While your document is open, go to the File menu and choose "Print."

3   In the Print dialog box, click on the "Printer" menu and choose "Add Printer...," as shown below.

Go to Step 4 on the opposite page.

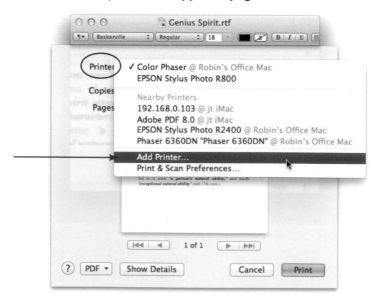

Or . . .

Exercise 5b: Use the Print & Scan system preferences to add a printer.

1   Turn on the printer you want to add to the List. Wait until it is fully warmed up (wait until it stops making noise and the green light is not flashing).

2   From the Apple menu, choose "System Preferences...." Single-click the "Print & Scan" icon.

Print & Scan

3   On the left side, at the bottom of the "Printers" pane, click the **+** button to get a menu; choose "Add Other Printer or Scanner...."

    Go to Step 4, below.

4   Both methods described on these two pages will open the printer list, as shown below. This list shows you the printers the Mac knows about already. Your Mac is aware of the most common printers and already has the "drivers" it needs to print to them.

    However, as I mentioned earlier, if you bought some fancy or expensive printer, be sure to install the software that came with it before you try to add it or print to it.

5   Single-click the name of the printer you want to use, then click the "Add" button.

6   That printer is now added to the list and you will be able to choose it in the Print dialog box.

Page setup

Get in the habit of checking the **Page Setup** option in the File menu. Page Setup is a dialog box where you can set specifications for printing the document—use these in conjunction with the individual Print dialog box specifications, as shown on the following pages. Below is a sample Page Setup box.

If you have several printers in your list, use the "Format for" menu to choose the one you plan to print to so the Mac will find the specific details about it, like different paper sizes it can take, what kinds of color options, etc.

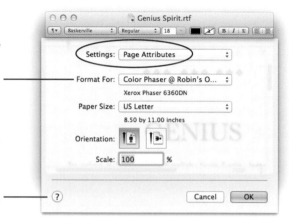

Click here for Help.

- **Paper Size:** This refers to the size of the paper that the document *will be printed on,* not the size of the page you are typing on. For instance, you might be creating a business card, but you can't put 2 x 3.5 paper through your printer—usually, the cards will be printed on regular letter-sized paper and cut out. If you have other-sized paper to use, choose it from this menu.

- **Orientation:** The Mac wants to know if the document should print normal (8.5 x 11) or sideways (11 x 8.5); also known as Tall or Wide, Portrait or Landscape.

- **Scale:** Enter a number here to enlarge or reduce the printed page. For instance, enter 50% to print your work at half size. Remember, half of an 8.5 x 11 is 4.25 x 5.5—you must halve *both* directions. On paper, this looks like the image is ¼ the original size; it isn't—it's half of both the horizontal *and* the vertical.

Reducing an image reduces it in both directions, not just one.

Once you have successfully added your printer to the list, you can print merrily away. On these next few pages are explanations of the various printing options you have. You will see different print dialog boxes depending on which printer you are connected to, and the dialog boxes within different applications will look slightly different from what you see here, but basically all you need to do is answer the questions they ask.

Most applications have a special menu option for specifications particular to that application. For instance, below are the options for printing from TextEdit; you can see that your options are very different from those in Address Book on the following page.

Print specifications

Application-specific options

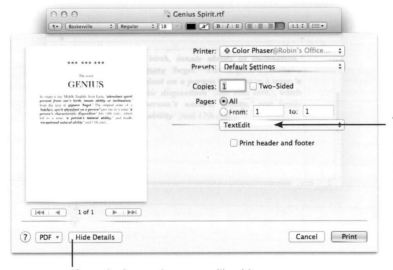

This shows the name of the application; single-click this menu to get other standard printing features.

If you don't see a large pane like this, this button probably says, "Show Details." Click it to view all the options for printing your document.

—continued

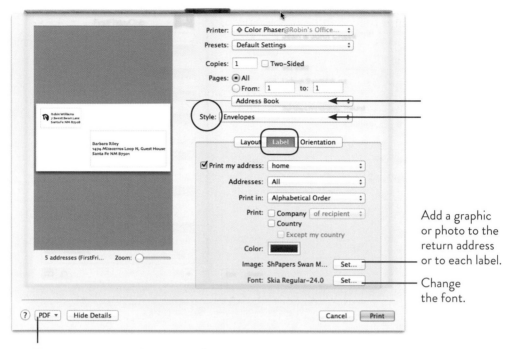

Create a PDF of any file; you can send it to others and it will look the same to them as it does to you.

This is one of the Print dialog panes for Address Book. Be sure to poke around in here and see all the options!

Under "Style," you'll find Mailing Labels, Envelopes (all sizes), Lists, and Pocket Address Book pages for putting into your Day-Timer® (if you still use a paper one).

Each of those styles gives you more options of what to include, how to set up the layout, color of ink to print, and so much more.

Add a graphic or photo to the return address or to each label.

Change the font.

See a preview   You might want to see a full-sized preview of all the pages of your job before you print, especially if you've made some specific settings. It's easy to do:

1 Click the "PDF" button in the bottom-left of the Print dialog box, shown circled above.

2 Choose "Open PDF in Preview" from that menu. This opens your document in the application called Preview and shows you what it will look like when printed.

3 If the job looks great, just click the "Print" button in the bottom-right of the Preview window.

If you want to make changes, click the "Cancel" button in the bottom-right of the Preview window to go back to the Print dialog box.

Very often you will not need to go beyond this first dialog box, where you can always choose **how many copies** to print and which **pages to print.**

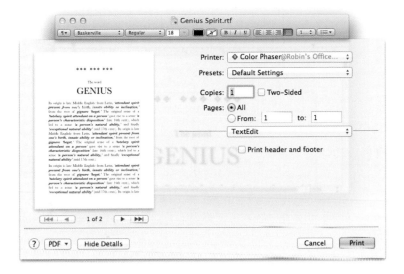

- **Copies:** Type in the number of copies you want to print.

- **Collated:** If you're printing more than one copy of a multi-page document, you can make the printer collate the copies—it will print all the pages of one set, then print the next set. If you *don't* click collate, you will get, for instance, five copies of page 1, five copies of page 2, five copies of page 3, etc. Keep in mind that it takes a bit longer for the printer to collate than to print multiple copies of one page at a time.

- **Pages: All** or **From __ to __:** You can choose to print *all* of the pages contained in your document, or just pages 3 through 12 (or whatever your choice is, of course).

  If you want to print just page 3, for example, type 3 in both boxes.

  If you don't know the number of the last page, enter something like "999" and the printer will print to the end.

  Choose **All** to override any numbers in the **From/to** boxes.

  In this dialog box, you cannot print non-consecutive pages, such as pages 3, 7, and 11 (you'll have to print those pages individually). If you use a page layout or other more sophisticated application, you will have the option to print non-consecutive pages.

Layout Choose **Layout** (from the menu circled below) when you want to print multiple pages on one sheet of paper. This is handy when you have, for instance, a presentation to give and you want to create handouts for your audience so they can follow along. Or it can help you see your overall project at a glance so you can get a better idea of how things are working together (or not).

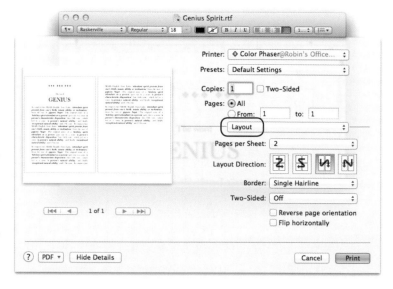

In this example, I have chosen two pages per sheet, a layout direction of top to bottom, and a single hairline border around each individual miniature page.

- **Pages per Sheet:** Choose how many pages of your document you want to see on each printed sheet of paper. Every page will be reduced to fit, of course.

- **Layout Direction:** Click a layout to determine how the pages are arranged on the sheet. In the example above, the third layout is clicked.

- **Border:** Choose one of the four border options so each page will be clearly defined on the printed sheet.

  You can only **print two-sided** (automatically) if you have bought a two-sided printer and installed its software. If your printer is not capable, that option will be gray.

In **color inkjet printers,** the type of paper you specify and put in the printer makes a remarkable difference in the finished image. A low-quality mode with cheap paper makes an image look worse than in the newspaper comic strip. But photo-quality paper with a high-quality mode can make the same image look like a photograph you had enlarged at a photo studio. Use the **Print Settings** to specify the paper ("Media Type") you have ready in the printer, plus the quality of your finished product.

Printer-specific options

Your "Print Settings" might not look exactly like the ones shown. Read the manual for your particular printer to learn all the details about every option.

The chosen printer in this example is a Color Phaser. The options for your printer might be different.

Find the "Printer Features" or "Image Quality" settings to adjust the printed image.

Some of the options will change as you choose different paper or print quality.

Tips for printing photographs:

- Use "photo quality" paper.
- From the "Media Type" or "Paper Type" menu, choose the paper that best describes the type you put into the printer.
- Choose the highest quality printing option.

Your printer has a manual that will help you choose specifications for the best printing. Be sure to read it!

Using the print queue window

You have a **print queue window** for each printer that you have added to your Printer List. A "print queue" is a lineup or sequence of jobs waiting to print. With this window you can control your print jobs, delete jobs, cancel them, queue them up for printing later, and more.

Control your print jobs

Below you see the print queue window where you manage your printing.

The name in the title bar of the window is the name of the printer that is printing these particular files. When this window (shown below) is visible, you have new menu items in the menu bar at the top of your monitor. The following describes things you can do using the menus or the icons in the toolbar.

To display the window shown above:

1 As soon as you click the "Print" button, a printer icon appears on the right side of the Dock.

2 Single-click that icon to get the printer job window shown above.

Also, see page 105 for a tip on how to get the printer job window (the print queue) at any time, even if you're not printing yet.

To control printing of individual documents and also of the entire printer:

- Single-click the Printer icon in the Dock while your document is in the process of printing (as explained on the opposite page); this brings up the print queue window.

    If you tell a document to print and it doesn't print, and you keep telling it to print over and over again, open this window and you'll see all of those documents waiting in line to print, just like you told them (see the next page).

    To fix the queue, first select the duplicate job names and click the "Delete" button, then figure out what's wrong: Is there one job clogging up the printer (maybe it's too big or the paper is the wrong size) and so the others are merely waiting, or have the jobs been paused? (Read on.) When you have fixed the problem, print the piece again.

This tiny exclamation point means the print queue has been stopped or paused and your job will not print.

You'll also see a symbol on the printer icon in the Dock if the queue is on hold or paused.

- **STOP ONE JOB from printing:** In the print queue window, click once on the name of a document in the list, then click the "Hold" button (or go to the Jobs menu at the top of the screen and choose "Hold Job"). This does not *delete* the job from the queue—it just puts it on hold.

- **STOP ALL DOCUMENTS from printing:** If the jobs are in the process of printing, find the icon in the toolbar labeled "Pause Printer." Single-click it to stop the entire lineup of documents waiting to print. While it is stopped, you can delete jobs, print an individual job, go to lunch, etc.

—continued

If you try to print several times and nothing goes through, check to make sure the jobs have not been paused! You'll know the queue has been paused because the icon in the toolbar will be labeled "Resume Printer." Plus, if you see an exclamation point in the Print dialog box, as shown on the previous page, that means the queue has been paused.

- **RESUME printing one job:** If a job has been put on hold, select its name in the job window. Then click the "Resume" button (or go to the Jobs menu and choose "Resume Job").

- **START ALL THE DOCUMENTS to print:** If the queue has been paused, the icon in the toolbar is labeled "Resume Printer," as shown below. Single-click this icon to start the printing process for the entire lineup of documents. Or select one or more documents, go to the Jobs menu, and choose "Resume Job."

This tells you what's going on.

This is the print queue.

This is the toolbar.

- **CANCEL a print job:** In the print queue window, click once on a document name to select it, then hit the Delete button in the toolbar (or go to the Jobs menu and choose "Delete Job").

  You can select more than one job to delete: Hold down the Command key and click each document name you want to delete. Then hit the Delete button.

- **CREATE A QUEUE:** If you want to send several print jobs to the printer, but you don't want to print them right now, put them in a queue: First open the print queue window and click the icon to "Pause Printer." Then, in your application, send as many jobs as you like to print. Each one will tell you that printing has been stopped and ask if you want to put this job in the queue. Click "Add to Queue."

  Later, when you're ready, click the button to "Resume Printer" (or use the Dock menu, as shown to the left— Control-click or right-click on the icon), and they will all print one after the other.

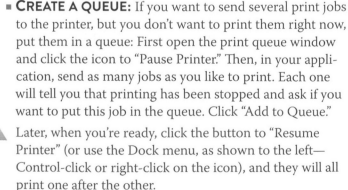

While the printer is in the process of printing, a **printer icon** appears in the **Dock,** then disappears when the job is finished. If you print regularly, though, it comes in handy to have the printer utility more easily accessible—you can keep it permanently in the Dock.

Keep your printer icon in the Dock

One way to make the icon stay in your Dock is to wait until the next time you print. You'll see the icon in the Dock. While it's there, *press* it (don't click!) and you'll get a menu; choose "Options," and then from its submenu, choose "Keep in Dock." The printer utility will stay there even after the printing is done (also see below).

If you don't want to wait until the next time you print, you can open the print queue window at any time through the System Preferences:

1 From the Apple menu, choose "System Preferences...."

2 Single-click the "Print & Scan" icon.

3 Choose a printer from the left hand pane.

4 Click the button to "Open Print Queue...."
   The printer job window, or print queue, will appear.

Another way to put the printer icon in the Dock:

While the Print & Scan system preferences (above) is open, drag the printer icon from the left pane; drag it down to the Dock and drop it in.

Remember. . .

- **Save your document** with a memorable name as soon as you start working on it.
- **SOS:** Save Often, Sweetie! Use the keyboard shortcut (Command S) to save every few minutes.

  sos is *Rule Number One* on the Mac.
- If you keep sending a job to print and **nothing comes out,** check the printer job window—the jobs are probably on hold or they are just waiting for a slow job to finish printing. See pages 102–104.

Close, Quit & Trash

There are three tasks you will constantly repeat while working on your Mac: You will **close documents** you have created or opened; you will **quit applications;** and you'll **trash files** you don't need anymore. Each task is incredibly easy.

This chapter uses the document you saved in Chapter 7. If you didn't do those exercises, open a new TextEdit document, save it, and type several paragraphs in it so you can work with the exercises in this chapter.

In this chapter

Close vs. Quit 108
    Unsaved changes 109
Close a document. 110
Quit an application 112
    Shortcut 113
    Force Quit 113
    Quit applications upon Log Out,
      Restart, and Shut Down. 114
Trash a file 115
    More ways to trash files 116
Also Try This 117
    Remove an item from the Trash. 117
Remember. 118

Close versus Quit

At first it seems a bit confusing—what's the big deal, **quitting** or **closing?** Either way, you're finished, right? Wrong.

Essentially, this is what happens: Say you open an *application* like your word processor—that is comparable to putting a typewriter on your office desk. Then you start a new *document*—that is comparable to putting a piece of paper in the typewriter.

When you choose "Close" from the File menu, that is comparable to taking the piece of paper (the document) out of the typewriter. The typewriter (the application), though, is still on the desk! On a computer, both the desk and the "typewriter" are rather invisible so you might think the typewriter (the application) is gone.

But the typewriter—the word processor application—stays on the desk (in the computer's **memory,** called RAM) until you physically put it away. When you choose "Quit" from the File menu, that is comparable to putting the typewriter away.

You can leave lots of applications open for weeks at a time, but you should **save** each of those documents regularly!

If you plan to edit movies or huge photos, you'll need a lot more memory than what comes with a Mac (more memory can be added at any time and is the most efficient way to make your Mac more productive and useful). But if all you're doing is word processing and sending email and surfing the web, the amount that comes with the machine is probably fine for a long time.

To find out how much memory is in your Mac, go to the Apple menu and choose "About This Mac."

Click here to put this panel away.

This says there are 4 gigabytes of memory (RAM) in this Mac.

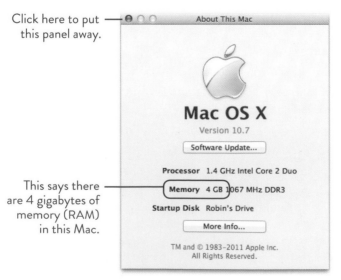

Note: A gigabyte is 1024 megabytes, and a megabyte is 1024 kilobytes, and a kilobyte is 1024 bytes, and it takes 1 byte to make a standard character on the screen, like the letter "A."

And because I know you really want to know, 1 byte is made of 8 bits.

And that's as small as it gets.

If a document title bar has the word "Edited" to the right of the name (as shown below), that means it has **unsaved changes,** meaning you made changes to the document since the last time you saved it (if ever). Perhaps you wrote more, fixed a typo, or changed the typeface.

Unsaved changes

Apple applications in Lion will automatically save the document when you close it, but don't count on all applications doing this yet! Get in the habit of saving often.

Exercise 1: Save your document.

Because Rule Number One on the Mac is "Save Often, Sweetie," (sos) let's just make sure the document you're working on is **saved.** If you don't have a document open, first create a new one in TextEdit, as explained in Chapter 6. Then:

1 Look at the title bar in your document window. Does it say "Edited"? That means, as you know by now, that the latest changes haven't been saved.

   If it doesn't say "Edited," type another word and you'll see it appear.

2 Save the document right now: Just press Command S. You'll see the word "Edited" go away.

   Always save your document before you close it. In fact, every few minutes press Command S to save your latest changes.

Also see pages 90–91 to learn about versions of a document and how to browse and restore them.

Close
a document

When you are finished working on a document for the moment, you can **close that document window** in a number of ways:

- **Either** click the red button in the upper-left corner of the document window.

- **Or** choose "Close" from the File menu.

- **Or** in most applications, the keyboard shortcut to close a document is **Command W,** just like closing a Finder **W**indow.

Whichever method you use, you are simply closing the *document* window (putting away the paper), while the *application* (the software program) is still open. You still see the menu belonging to the application, even though the rest of your screen may look just like your Desktop, and you might even see windows that belong to other applications or to the Desktop!

Exercise 2: Close your document and open another.

1 Single-click the document window just to make sure it's the active window.

2 Do any one of the three options listed above to close the document. Don't click anywhere else yet!

   If you have more than one document open, close the other one(s).

3 Notice that even though the document window is gone, the menu bar across the top of the screen still says "TextEdit" (see the opposite page). That's because you closed the *document,* but you are still in the *application.*

4 Single-click anywhere on the Desktop.

5 Look at the menu bar now—where it said "TextEdit" a second ago, it says "Finder." That's because as soon as you clicked the Desktop, you popped out of the application TextEdit, and now the Finder/Desktop is *active.*

6 **Go back to TextEdit:** Notice the TextEdit icon in the Dock has a blue bubble light beneath it; that's because it's still open, even though you can't see it.

   Single-click the TextEdit icon in the Dock, and your menu bar will change to show that TextEdit is now active.

7 **Create a new document** in TextEdit: From the "File" menu, choose "New."

   Type a paragraph or two, and save it into the Documents folder with the name "Toss This" because you're going to throw it away soon.

This Finder window is NOT active; its buttons and toolbar are gray.

You can tell by the menu bar that TextEdit is the active application.

Notice there are **two windows open,** a document window and a Finder window. The document window is "active"; you can tell because the three buttons in its upper-left are in color.

This scene is my Desktop image. You can change your Desktop too, if you like; see page 171.

Even though I closed the document, TextEdit is still active—you can see its name in the menu bar.

If I were to single-click the Finder window (its buttons are gray at the moment because it is **not** active), that Finder window would "come forward" and be active, and the menu bar would change to "Finder" instead of "TextEdit."

TIP: If the blue bubble lights do not appear under an open application, that means they are turned off in the system preferences. **To turn them back on,** go to the Apple menu and choose "Dock," then choose "Dock Preferences...." Check the box to "Show indicator lights for open applications." To close the preferences, click its red dot.

111

Quit an application

To quit an application, you must choose the Quit command. This command is always in the application menu (the one with the name of the active application), and "Quit" is always the very last item. In every application you can use the keyboard shortcut instead: **Command Q.**

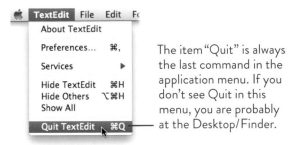

The item "Quit" is always the last command in the application menu. If you don't see Quit in this menu, you are probably at the Desktop/Finder.

If you haven't saved all of your changes in any of the open documents when you choose to quit, the application will either ask if you want to save them at this point, or (if it is an app made for Lion) it will go ahead and save it without telling you.

This is what each button in the above dialog box will do:

- Single-click the **Don't Save** button if you decide at this point that you don't want to save the latest changes (*or* the entire document *if* you've never named it).

  You can use the keyboard shortcut Command D instead of actually clicking the "Don't Save" button. In some applications, you can just hit the letter D.

- Single-click **Cancel** (or press Command Period) to return to your document without saving any changes or quitting.

- If you single-click **Save** and you haven't yet saved the document with a name, you'll get the "Save As…" dialog box (pages 88–89) to name the document before quitting. You can hit the Return or Enter key *instead* of clicking the Save button.

Quit when you are finished working in the application for the day. Once you quit, the application is removed from the computer's memory.

Alternatively, feel free to leave the application open for days on end, while you put your computer to sleep at night (see page 179). If the application starts acting a little funny or sluggish after a long while of staying open, quit and then open it back up again.

Exercise 3: Quit TextEdit.

1 Make sure TextEdit is the active application: If you don't see "TextEdit" in your menu bar, as circled on page 111, single-click its icon in the Dock.

2 From the File menu, choose "Quit."
Or use the keyboard shortcut instead, Command Q.

Notice there is no longer a blue bubble under the TextEdit icon in the Dock.

There is a sweet little **shortcut to quit.** You don't even have to open the application to do this. Just *press* (don't click) the application's icon in the Dock. In the pop-up menu that appears, choose "Quit."

Shortcut

Press an open application icon to get this menu.

Or you can **Control-click** (or right-click) to get this menu.

Sometimes an application acts so goofy that you have no choice but to **force quit.** For instance, you might see the spinning ball for much too long, or things just stop working in the application, or other weird stuff. And then when you try to quit, you can't!

Force Quit

If you have to force an application to quit, do one of these things:

- Press Command Option Escape (esc). A small dialog box appears; make sure the application name is chosen, then click the blue button to "Force Quit."
- Hold down the Option key and *press* (don't click) the Dock icon. The command "Quit," as shown above, turns into "Force Quit."

You can't force quit the Finder, but you can "Relaunch" the Finder, which sometimes helps clean things up a bit if it starts exhibiting puzzling behavior.

113

Quit applications upon Log Out, Restart, and Shut Down

Generally, when you choose to Log Out, Restart, or Shut Down (all from the Apple menu), the Mac will **automatically quit** all open applications for you. (An exception is when you have enabled "fast user switching" and are logging out so another user can log in; see my bigger book, *Mac OS X Lion: Peachpit Learning Series*.)

If you have documents still open that have changes that need to be saved, you will get a message for some, giving you the opportunity to save them (if it's an Apple application built for Lion, it will save the document for you, even in you haven't). This is a great option if you tend to leave lots of applications open—at the end of the week, instead of taking the time to quit each individual application, just Shut Down and they will all quit anyway.

This is the message you'll get if you choose to Log Out (from the Apple menu) while applications are still open. Click the "Log Out" button to start the process.

Check the button to "Reopen windows when logging back in," and all applications that had open windows in them will automatically reopen when you log back in. In Apple apps, such as TextEdit, even your unsaved changes will still be there when you get back.

Take note! If you have a lot of applications open, don't choose "Shut Down" or "Log Out" or "Restart" and then walk away from your computer! Wait until you see the gray screen, because if there is an unsaved document anywhere on your Mac that it can't save for you, a message will pop up asking you to save it. If you aren't there to deal with it, the Shut Down process (or Log Out or Restart process) times out and your computer just sits there, patiently waiting for you to come back, which might be days.

To put something in the Trash, press-and-drag an icon over to the Trash can (actually, it looks like a wire wastebasket). When the basket turns dark, as shown below, let go and the file will drop inside. Don't let go of the file before the basket turns dark! If you find a bunch of garbage hanging around outside the Trash or sitting in the Dock, it's because you didn't wait for it to turn dark—you just set the trash down *next to* the basket.

The trick is that the **tip of the pointer** must touch the Trash basket! Whether you are putting one file in the Trash or whether you have selected several icons and are dragging them all together to the Trash, **the tip of the pointer** is what selects the wastebasket. The shadows of the objects have nothing to do with it—forget those shadows you see trailing along—just make sure the tip of the pointer touches the basket and highlights it (turns it dark). *Then* let go.

Anything you put in the Trash basket stays there, even if you turn off the computer, until you consciously empty the Trash (explained on the following page).

Trash a file

RedDog.gif

You can see the original file (the top one), plus the shadow that is pulled by the pointer (over the Trash basket). When the **tip of the pointer** touches the basket, the basket high-lights, or turns dark. That means you can let go.

The paper in the basket is an obvious **visual clue** that there is something in the garbage.

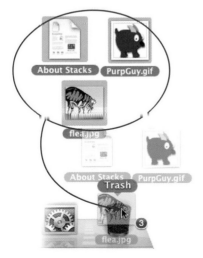

Here you can see I selected three files. (I held down the Command key and clicked each one.)

Then I **let go** of the Command key, dragged **one** of those selected files to the Trash, and the rest followed.

You can see all three shadows of the files, but notice where the pointer is. It's that **tip of the pointer, not** the shadows of the icons, that selects the Trash so the files can drop in.

115

TIP: If you empty the Trash and tragically realize that you threw away your only copy of something very important, there is software and there are technicians who can often bring back your information. So if you lose something important, call your local guru, power user, or user group. In the meantime, don't turn off your computer or create new files.

In general, however, assume that when you toss something in the Trash, then empty the Trash, it's gone.

Exercise 4: Throw a file in the Trash basket.

1 If you did Exercise 2, you have a file in your Documents folder named "Toss This."

Find that file so it's visible (single-click the Documents icon in the Sidebar, then scroll if necessary to find it).

2 Press (don't click) that document icon and drag it to the Trash basket.

3 Make sure the tip of the pointer is positioned on the Trash basket, so the icon turns dark, then let go.

4 **To empty the Trash:** *Press* (don't click) the Trash icon. A little menu pops up that says "Empty Trash." Select that item and let go.

You can also Control-click (or right-click) to get this menu.

More ways to trash files

There are several other ways to **move an item to the Trash** besides physically dragging a file and dropping it in the basket.

- Select the item (click it once).
  From the File menu, choose "Move to Trash."

- *Or* select the item (click it once).
  Press Command Delete.

- *Or* hold down the Control key (not the Command key) and single-click a file you want to throw away. A contextual menu pops up (as shown below) and gives you, among other things, the option to move that item to the Trash. Choose it.

Also Try This

To remove an item from the Trash *before* you have emptied it, single-click on the Trash icon. It opens up to a window, just like any other window! So if you decide you want that item you just threw away, you can go get it. But don't forget—you can only get items back from the Trash if you have not emptied the Trash!

Remove an item from the Trash

- If you change your mind directly after you throw something away, press Command Z (the "Undo" command), and the item you just put in the Trash will be instantly put back where it came from.

  Remember that Command Z acts as Undo for *the very last action you did;* that is, if you put a second file in the Trash, it is the second file that will be put back, not the first one.

- Open the Trash window (single-click its Dock icon) to see the window shown below. Select the file you want to put back, and from the File menu, choose "Put Back." *Or* press Command Delete.

- You can always open the Trash window and drag the file out of the window and put it back where it belongs, as long as you have not emptied the Trash yet.

The Trash basket opens to a window. Drag any file out and put it wherever you want.

You might want to open another window (Command N) so you can move items from this Trash window to another window, or drag an item out of the window pane and drop it on one of the icons in your Sidebar, such as your Documents folder.

Remember. . .

- The command to **Close** will close just that *active* window; it does not close the application.

- The command to **Quit** will quit the active application. If you have unsaved documents still open, you will be asked if you want to save them first. Thank goodness.

- Anything you put in the **Trash** will stay there, even if you turn off the computer or if the power goes out, until you choose to empty the trash.

Get Connected 9

If your Mac is already connected to the Internet, skip this entire chapter! If you just turned on your Mac and it's asking you strange questions about your Internet Service Provider or your connection method, read this chapter before you continue with the setup. **OR** skip the setup and come back to this chapter **when you're ready to make a connection.**

In this chapter

You need an Internet Service Provider . . . 120

You need a modem. 120

Step by step: What to do. 122

Information you need before you start . . . 123

Getting ready to set up 124

    Use Network preferences 124

Set up your broadband connection 125

Connect to the Internet 127

Set the service order 127

Remember. 128

You need an Internet Service Provider

If you are already connected to the Internet, skip this entire chapter!

So how do you get to the Internet and the web? You need a computer (or a mobile device such as an iPad) and a browser. Your Mac, of course, is your computer. A browser is a software application and you've got this on your Mac—it's called Safari. Plus you need an Internet Service Provider. And you need a modem.

You see, you can't hook into the Internet directly from your own computer—you must go through an **Internet Service Provider (ISP).** From your home or business, you need to *pay* a provider to provide you with a connection to the Internet. You pay them; they connect you to the Internet.

Your local phone company probably provides DSL (digital subscriber line) service for the Internet, and your cable TV company probably provides cable service for the Internet. There are probably several Internet Service Providers in your area. There are also a couple of national providers that can set you up with a connection. Ask around your town for the names of the favored providers.

An Internet Service Provider will also give you one or more email addresses.

> **Note:** But not everyone who gives you an email address also provides an Internet connection! For instance, you can get a free email account at Gmail.com or yahoo.com or Apple.com, but these services are not *providers;* they cannot get you connected to the Internet. They just provide you with an email address to use once you get connected.

Before you get connected, *you must first establish a relationship with a provider* ("establish a relationship" = pay them money). The provider will give you the information necessary to continue with the setup process, as explained on the following pages. You can set up your connection at any time; that is, if you are ready when you first turn on your Mac to set it up, you can do that. Or you can skip the Internet setup at that time and do it next week or next month or next year, as explained on the following pages.

You need a modem

Before you can get connected in the first place, you need a **modem,** which is a box-like device that transforms the data sent between computers. The kind of modem you need depends on how you plan to connect to the Internet.

Most people connect through a **high-speed broadband modem;** your ISP will provide you with that modem. *If you have a choice,* *go for the **broadband**—it's always on, it's fast, and your Mac relies on broadband for many of its features.*

Some people are limited to a **dial-up phone modem** that uses your phone line. If you have a very old Mac (older than about six years), this modem might be built into it, but for more recent Macs you will have to buy an *external modem,* which means it plugs into the outside of the Mac. The directions in this chapter are for broadband; if you must use a dial-up, your Internet Service Provider will get you connected.

This is an external modem for a Mac. It plugs into a USB port.

> **Note:** If you want to **fax** from your Mac, you must use a phone modem, even if you have a broadband connection. Plug the telephone cable into the modem port and into a wall jack or telephone. A fax will not go through the broadband connection—it must go through the phone line. A dial-up modem ties up your phone line.

This icon identifies the USB port.

> **To fax,** open your document and hit Command P to print. In the bottom-left corner, click the "PDF" button. Choose "Fax PDF...."

For a **high-speed broadband** "always-on" connection such as DSL, ISDN, cable, T1, T3, or satellite, you will need a special modem specifically for that service. The company that provides the broadband service also provides the modem. You connect to this modem with an **Ethernet** cable, which you'll plug into the Ethernet port on your Mac. The connectors (the things on the ends) on an Ethernet cable look very similar to a standard phone cable, but a little larger. The Ethernet port looks very similar to a telephone jack, but a little larger.

This is the Ethernet port on your Mac; it looks like a large phone jack. DO NOT plug a phone line into this—it won't work!

You will use an Ethernet cable to connect your Mac to a broadband modem.

When you're connected through a broadband modem, you just open your browser and you're on the web. You open your email application and get your email. **Broadband is always on.**

More than one computer in the house can connect at the same time with one broadband connection.

Most new computers, especially laptops, have **wireless** cards built in and can connect to any wireless connection. Now, your *computer* connection might be wireless, but there still needs to be a modem in the house or office that connects with wires to the Internet Service Provider. Often the modem itself provides a wireless signal. Be sure to tell the installer that you want to be able to use the wireless signal.

Step by step: What to do

Below are the basic **steps** to follow to get yourself connected to the Internet so you can browse the web and do email.

1 Choose an **Internet Service Provider,** call them up, and pay your money (see the previous pages).

2 Get your **modem** hooked up. Your service provider will hook up the modem for you, but in our experience, they won't always get your Mac set up to work with it. If you have a Mac-knowledgeable technician who does that for you, that's great—you're done. Skip to the next chapter.

3 Get the **setup information** from your provider. See the next two pages.

4 **Either** walk through the **setup process** if you're turning on your Mac for the first time, and fill in the information (pages 125–127 show screens similar to those you'll see during the initial setup).

   Or do it later: During the initial setup process, click the button that says you'll connect later. After you get your Mac all put together, then use the Network preferences. (See pages 125–127.)

5 After you've set up the preferences, you're **ready to connect.** On a **broadband account,** wired or wireless, just open your browser or email program; see page 127.

6 On a broadband account, you don't need to disconnect when you're finished. Just leave it on and connect to the world at any moment. It's so great.

Whether you walk through the Setup Assistant the first time you turn on your Mac, *or* you decide to do it later, there is **information you need to have** from your Internet Service Provider (ISP) or network administrator.

Have the information your provider gave you before you begin:

- User account/ISP account name and password.
- Email address and password *(which might or might not be the same as your account name and password— often it is not!).*
- If you are on a local area network (LAN) in a large corporation or school, ask your system administrator for the pertinent information.

Write this information down! I guarantee you will need it again someday! Make sure you differentiate between your ISP account and its password—and your email address and its password. And don't forget to write down every password as well and keep your list in a safe place (that is, don't keep your list of passwords near your computer because if your computer is stolen, the passwords will probably get stolen too).

To add an existing email account during the initial setup process, you will need:

- Your email address at that account.
- **Incoming mail server name.** This will be something like mail.myDomainName.com *or* pop.myDomainName.com.

  This is not always the same as your provider's name. For instance, I own the domain "ratz.com" and I get email there, so my *incoming mail server* name for that particular email account is "mail.ratz.com." But my *provider* is comcast.net.

- **Outgoing mail server (SMTP).** SMTP stands for Simple Mail Transfer Protocol, but who cares. This information will look something like **smtp.myProvider.com.**

  The SMTP is *always* the name of your Internet Service Provider (see the caveat on the following page) because that is where your email gets sent *out* from. No matter how many different email accounts you have *coming in,* your *outgoing* mail server is always the one you are paying

Information you need before you start

I keep a small Rolodex file of account names and passwords for online accounts, email, catalogs, libraries, Apple, Adobe, eBay, airlines, bookstores, etc.

If you choose not to set up your email account in the initial setup process when you first get your Mac, you can always do it later. See Chapter 11.

money to for your Internet connection; it is always your service provider.

> **Caveat: Technically, that's not quite true!** You actually *can* use a different SMTP, such as me.com or gmail.com, but I guarantee you will have fewer problems if you use your provider's SMTP for every account. When you know you need a different SMTP, perhaps for traveling or other purposes, call your provider and ask what your options are for outgoing mail while you are away from your home/office connection.
>
> Or go to **smtp.com** and buy a temporary SMTP account to use while traveling. It's great.

POP: Post Office Protocol

IMAP: Internet Message Access Protocol

- **Account type: IMAP or POP.** Most email accounts are POP accounts. Services like America Online and MobileMe (which is being phased out as I write this) are IMAP accounts. Ask your provider to be sure; if you can't get hold of them, choose POP for now and you can always change it later once you find out.

Getting ready to set up

You can get connected to the Internet during the setup process the first time you turn on your new Mac, or you can do it at any time after your computer is up and running. The questions are the same either way. Apple has made it so easy to connect to the Internet that you could be surfing the web in just a few clicks.

Before you start the process, make sure your modem is plugged into the wall appropriately (depending on what kind of modem you have), and that there is a cable connecting the modem to your Mac. If you plan to connect to an existing wireless network, make sure it is turned on and listed in the Wi-Fi menu that's in the menu bar at the top of your screen.

Use Network preferences

If you're turning on your Mac for the first time, it will ask you similar questions to the ones you see following this page. **If your computer is already set up,** use the Network preferences as explained on the following pages.

You will also need to use these Network preferences when you decide to switch providers, when you upgrade to a broadband connection from a dial-up, when you connect your Macs over Ethernet to share files, when things go wrong, etc.

As I mentioned on the previous page, the questions are the same whether you are installing a new operating system on your Mac, turning your Mac on for the first time right out of the box, or setting up the connection long after you've been using the computer. The windows look a little different, but the information is the same.

To open and use the Network preferences:

1 From the Apple menu, choose "System Preferences...," *or* click the System Preferences icon in the Dock.

2 Single-click the "Network" icon. The network status of your current connection is displayed in the left-hand pane of this window, as shown below. You may see more than one "service" possibility in this list.

Set up your broadband connection

System Preferences icon in the Dock.

Network icon in System Preferences.

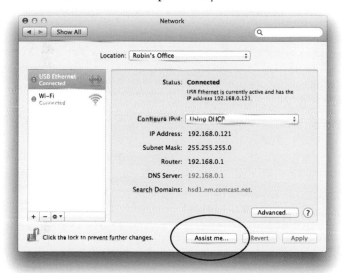

Your Mac compiles this list depending on your computer and what kinds of cables and hardware (like modems) you have attached.

3 **To let your Mac guide you** through the setup process, click the "Assist me..." button, shown circled above. A little sheet drops down, shown below: Click "Assistant...."

You will be guided through a series of simple screens in which you'll choose or enter information, as shown on the next page.

These are examples of the helpful screens that guide you through the connection process.

The location name tells **you** which connection you're using, in case you have more than one. This name will appear in the Apple menu under "Location" so you can choose it from there.

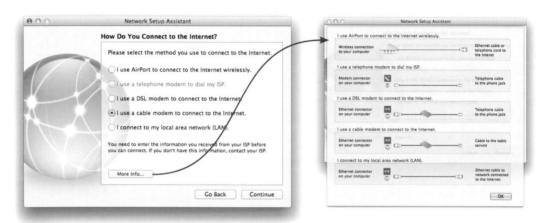

If you're not sure about what kind of connection you have, click the "More Info..." button for a description of the possible services.

If you are in an office that is connected to the Internet through an ISDN, T1, or T3 line, your Mac is not **directly** connected to an incoming modem box, so you will choose "local area network (LAN)."

With a cable connection, DSL, or a LAN, that's all you need to do!

The **AirPort wireless** connection needs to know your password, if there is one, and assumes that someone has previously set up your AirPort.

If you have a **broadband account,** then you are already connected to the Internet. All you have to do is open a browser or your email application and there you are. It's fabulous.

You don't need to disconnect—broadband is "always on."

Some low-class broadband providers will make you go through a little connection process, like a dial-up, which defeats half the purpose of having a broadband connection. Try to find a company that doesn't do that.

Connect to the Internet

Here is an important **troubleshooting tip.** Your Mac follows a certain order in trying to establish a connection, and it might think you have several options for connecting (whether they are set up or not). If you're having trouble, you can change this order so the computer first tries to connect with your preferred service.

Set the service order

To change the connectivity order of services:

1 In the Network system preferences, single-click the Action menu icon, shown circled below. From the menu that drops down, choose "Set Service Order...."

2 The sheet you see below drops down from the toolbar. All the services are listed. *Press (don't click) the one you use to connect and drag it to the very top.* Click OK.

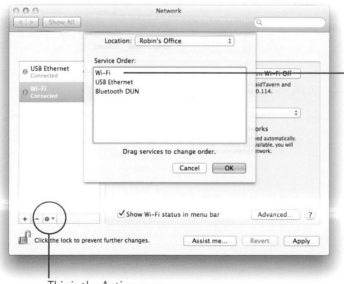

Drag your preferred service to the top of the list. Watch the dark line—when you let go, the service will land where the dark line is.

This is the Action menu.

Remember . . .

- If you have a **broadband** connection, you are *always* connected to the Internet (unless you use a crummy provider), and you can instantly open and use your browser or email program anytime you like, night or day.

Are ya ratty for the Net?

Surf the Web 10

Different things you do on your Macintosh require different applications. To browse the web, you'll use the software application called a **browser.** In your Dock, you have an icon for the browser called Safari.

This is the Safari icon that you should see in the Dock. If it's not there, you'll find it in your Applications folder.

You can view web pages in your browser, watch movies, hear music, print from your browser, and on and on. In this chapter, I'm going to give you some basic tips that will get you started right away.

In this chapter

What are web pages?	130
What is a web address?	130
If you want to connect right now	130
What are links?	131
Resize the text on a web page	132
Go back and forth from page to page	133
Open a new browser window	134
Check the Dock	134
Enter a web address	135
Shortcut to enter an address	136
Choose your Home page	137
Bookmarks	138
View bookmarks in Cover Flow	139
Put a web page link in your Dock	139
Check out the Top Sites page	140
Search tools	140
Important Point Number One	140
Important Point Number Two	140
Search using Google	141
Use Reader mode to remove clutter	142
Make a Reading list	143
Remember	144

The word "web" isn't capitalized since we don't capitalize other forms of communication such as radio, television, or telephone.

What are web pages?

The web is comprised of several billion individual **web pages.** These pages are quite the same as the pages you create in your word processor—in fact, many of them are created in word processors, and the code for most web pages can be viewed in a word processor.

The big deal about web pages is that they have "hypertext links"— text you click on to make another page appear in front of you. It's like this: Imagine that you could open a book to its table of contents and touch, say, "Chapter 3," and the page instantly transforms itself to Chapter 3. In Chapter 3, there is a reference to Greek mythology. You touch the words "Greek mythology," and a book about Greek mythology instantly appears in front of you, open to the page you want. As you're reading about Greek mythology, you see a reference to goddess worship, so you touch that reference and instantly that book appears in front of you, open to the page you want. That's what web pages do, that's what hypertext is. That's what's incredible.

What is a web address?

Even though there are several billion web pages on the Internet right now, every web page has its own **address,** just like every house in the country has an address of some sort. The address is sometimes called a **URL** (pronounced *you are ell*). When you get to page 135, you'll learn exactly how to enter a URL so you can view that page.

If you want to connect right now

You don't have to **connect to the Internet** and the web to read this chapter—you can skim through and get the gist of how to use your browser and the web.

But if you already have a **full-time broadband connection** (cable modem, DSL, ISDN, or T1 line) and want to connect so you can experiment in this chapter, all you need to do to get to the Internet is single-click the Safari browser icon in your Dock.

This is the browser that came with your Mac, called Safari. If you have a broadband (full-time) connection already set up, just single-click this icon to go to the web.

If you're **not connected at all** or if you have no idea how you are connected, please see the previous chapter.

Every web page has **links** on it. Single-click a link with your mouse and a new web page appears. A link might be text or it might be a graphic. If it's text, it often has an underline, or at least it's in a different color; if it's a graphic, it sometimes has a border around it. Even if the **visual clues** of the underline or the border are missing, you can always tell when something is a link because the pointer turns into a hand with a pointing finger, as shown to the right. Just run your mouse over the page *(without pressing the button down),* and you'll see the pointer turn into the browser hand whenever you "mouse over" a link.

What are links?

This is a typical "browser hand" that you'll see on a web page.

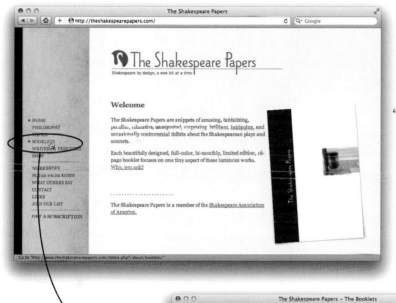

This is a typical web page. You can see the browser hand positioned over colored text, about to click the link to go to the "Booklets" page.

Not all links have underlines; the browser hand tells you what is a link.

When you click a link like the one circled above, "Booklets," the browser jumps to another page, in this case the page shown to the right. You can see there are links on this new page. You can click links for the rest of your life and still not have time to read everything.

That's the World Wide Web.

Exercise 1: Poke around some web pages.

1 Apple has set a default (an automatic action) for Safari that takes you to a particular web page (usually an Apple page) when you open Safari for the first time. That web page has lots of links. Just single-click any link on that page that interests you. Poke around for a while!

2 To go to pages you have previously visited, use the Back and Forward buttons, as shown on the opposite page.

3 To go to a particular page whose web address you know, see page 135 (try going to www.UrlsInternetCafe.com).

Resize the text on a web page Sometimes the text on a web page is too small to read easily. If so, just press the keyboard shortcut **Command +**, and the text will enlarge (that's the **+** key to the left of the Delete key). Press the same shortcut again to make the text even larger.

To make the text smaller, press **Command -** (that's the minus sign, to the left of the + key).

You see **buttons** in your **toolbar.** The ones you will use most often are "Back" and "Forward." The Back button, of course, takes you back through pages you have visited. Once you've gone back, then the Forward button appears so you can go forward again.

Go back and forth from page to page

Use these buttons to go back and forth through pages you have already seen.

Press the Back button (*hold* the mouse button down), and you'll get a menu that lists the pages you have been to. Just slide down and choose the one you want to see again.

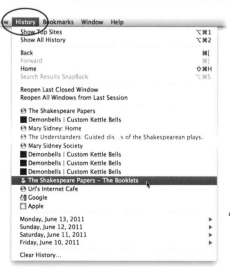

You can also use the **History menu** to go directly to pages you previously visited.

The **History menu** keeps track of every web page you've been to for the past month. You can change how long it hangs on to web pages—use the Preferences, found in the Safari menu. You can set Safari so it only keeps track for a day, a week, two weeks, or an entire year.

To eliminate everything from the History menu, scroll to the very bottom of the menu and choose "Clear History."

Open a new browser window

You can have lots and **lots of browser windows open.** This comes in handy when you really like a page, or maybe a page has several interesting links you want to follow, and when you go to another page you don't want this one to disappear. So instead of clicking the link to get another page, Control-click it (hold the *Control key* down, not the *Command key,* and click once). You will get a menu right there in the middle of the page, and one of the options is "Open Link in New Window." Choose that option—a new window with the new page will open *in front of* the previous window.

The Back button on the new page will be gray because, since this is a new window, it has nowhere to go back to. Your original page still retains all of the Back pages in its list.

Hold down the Control key and click a link to get a menu like this. The options in the menu differ depending on what you click.

Exercise 2: Open windows in tabs.

You can also use the "Window" menu in Safari to choose open pages.

1 Check to see if Safari is already set to open in tabs: Go to the Safari menu, choose "Preferences…," then click the "Tabs" icon. Make sure there *is* a check next to "⌘-click opens a link in a new tab." Close the preferences.

2 Open a page in a new **tab:** Command-click any link. That new page opens *behind* the existing page in a new tab—you can see the tab beneath the toolbar. Click the tab to open that window. You can have hundreds of tabbed windows open.

Check the Dock

When multiple, individual web pages are open (not tabbed pages), they can all be displayed in the **Dock pop-up menu.** Press the mouse on the Safari icon in the Dock, as shown below, and choose the page that you want to come forward.

Press on the Safari icon in the Dock.

To enter a web address, type it into the "Location" box at the **top** of the window, in the toolbar. **After you type it in,** hit Return or Enter to tell the browser to go find that page. Notice carefully in the illustrations below where the Location box is located!

This is where you type the web address (the URL).

DO NOT type a web address in this field!

(Well, it won't hurt anything, but it's silly to enter it here. This is the **search** field.)

This is where you type the web address (the URL).

DO NOT type a web address in this field!

Exercise 3: Enter a web address.

1 Select the text that is currently in the Location box (an easy way to do that is to press Command L).

2 Type a web address, such as **www.apple.com** (you don't have to type **http://**).

3 Hit the Return or the Enter key to go to the site. Voilà!

Shortcut to enter an address

And here's an extra-special **shortcut** you will love. On the Mac, you don't have to type in the entire ugly web address with the http:// and all. For one thing, you never need to type http://. So skip that part altogether. If the rest of the address is in this format, www.**something**.*com,* all you need to type is **something**. Really.

For instance, to go to http://www.**apple**.com, all you need to type is **apple**, then hit Return or Enter. The browser looks for a *.com* address with the name you entered, and if it finds one, it takes you there. The company.com part of the address is called the *domain.* (If the browser cannot find a web site with that domain name, it does a search for that topic and shows you the results of the search.)

If the address uses another domain identifier, such as *.org* or *.net* instead of *.com,* you'll have to type *.org* or *.net,* etc. And if the address has other slashes and stuff, you'll have to type everything after the domain.

Exercise 4: Use a web address shortcut.

1 In Safari, use the shortcut Command L. This highlights the Location box where you enter an address.

2 Type **apple**

3 Hit Return.

4 Try it with other names of companies who surely have their own web sites, such as Sears, NFL, Disney, etc. (And remember, you don't have to type capital letters, even if the address contains capital letters, until after the end of the domain. But *after* the domain slash, it is absolutely critical that you type capital letters or lowercase letters exactly as shown.)

http://www.TheUnderstanders.com/

You don't ever have to type this part.

In this area, it doesn't matter whether you type capitals or lowercase.

After this slash, you MUST type capitals or lowercase to exactly match the web address.

You can **choose your own Home page.** "Home" in a browser is the page you find yourself going to the most while you're surfing the web. For instance, I chose **Google.com** as my home page. John likes **News.Google.com** for instant access to news.

When you click the "Home" icon in the toolbar, Safari instantly displays the web page you have chosen as your home page.

Choose your Home page

This is the **Home** button. If you don't see it, follow **Step 6,** below.

This is the **Bookmarks Bar;** see the next page.

Exercise 5: Choose your Home page.

1 Single-click the blank area of a web page to make sure Safari is active.

2 From the Safari menu, choose "Preferences...."

3 Single-click the "General" icon in the toolbar.

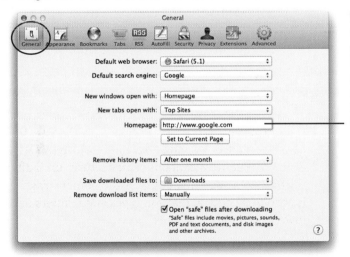

Whatever address you type in here will become your **"Home"** address. That is, whenever you click the Home button in the toolbar, or when you create a new Safari window, you will go to this page.

4 In the "Homepage" field, type the complete web address of the page you want as your Home page.
Or click "Set to Current Page" to make the current web page open in Safari as the Home page.

5 Click the red Close button in the top-left corner.

6 **If you don't have a Home button in your Safari toolbar, put it there:** From the View menu, choose "Customize Toolbar...." Drag the Home icon into the toolbar. Click the "Done" button.

7 Single-click that Home button in the Safari toolbar, and it takes you to the web page you specified.

Bookmarks

As you wander around the web, you'll run across web sites you really like and want to come back to. For these sites, make a **Bookmark:** Simply press Command D while viewing the page, *or* click the **+** button in the toolbar. You'll be asked to choose a location to store the bookmark and to set a bookmark name. Once you have a bookmark, that page shows up in the Bookmarks location you chose, and you can just choose it from that menu.

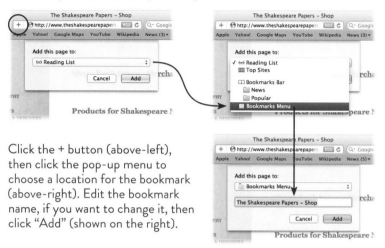

Click the + button (above-left), then click the pop-up menu to choose a location for the bookmark (above-right). Edit the bookmark name, if you want to change it, then click "Add" (shown on the right).

As you make lots of bookmarks, you'll need to organize them. Safari has fabulous tools for organizing your bookmarks, but this book is getting too big already—please see *Mac os x Lion: Peachpit Learning Series* for more details about bookmarks in Safari, as well as everything else you need to know about using this great browser.

Exercise 6: Make and use a bookmark.

1 Go to any page that you want to be able to find again quickly.

2 While viewing that page, press Command D, *or* go to the Bookmarks menu and choose "Add Bookmark…."

3 A little sheet drops down and asks you to name the bookmark: The name of the web page is already *selected (highlighted),* so just type to change the name.

It also asks you where to save it: From the little pop-up menu on that sheet, choose "Bookmarks Menu." *

4 Now go to a few other web pages, just clicking random links.

5 **To go to your bookmarked page,** single-click the Bookmarks menu, then slide down and choose the bookmark that you added just a minute ago.

*If you want instant access to favorite sites, go to the View menu and choose "Show Bookmarks Bar." Then choose to save the bookmark in the **"Bookmarks Bar."** The link will be put into that little bar above the web page, as shown on the previous page.

Safari can also display your bookmarks in a "cover flow" view. **To see all your bookmarks,** click the "Show all bookmarks" button on the left end of the Bookmarks Bar, circled below. You can make folders in which to store your bookmarks, drag them up or down to reorganize them, and search through them all.

View Bookmarks in Cover Flow

Search bookmarks.

Select the bookmark collection you want to show or search.

Click this ✚ sign to create a new folder in which to store bookmarks.

If you don't really want to see these covers, drag this "thumb" all the way up, as far as it will go.

Exercise 7: Put a link to a web page right in your Dock.

Put a web page link in your Dock

1 In Safari, go to the page you want to put in the Dock.

2 See that tiny icon to the left of the web address in the location box? Drag that tiny icon down to the *right* side of the dividing line in the Dock, then let go.

3 You'll get one of those springy-things in the Dock. Whenever you want to go to that page, just single-click the spring. If your browser is not open, this will open it.

Drag this icon and drop it in the Dock. You can also drop it on the Desktop.

When you hover over the icon with the mouse, you'll see the web page title.

Check out the Top Sites page

Safari keeps track of the sites that you return to over and over again and displays them in the "Top Sites" window. **To show the Top Sites window,** as seen below, single-click the tiny grid in the Bookmarks Bar, if it's showing (circled below-left), *or* go to the History menu and choose "Show Top Sites."

You **can** drag pages into different positions, but they are going to change anyway as you go to new sites (as you can see to the right).

Click the "Edit" button (it changed to "Done" above), and you'll get an **X** and pushpin on each page. Click the **X** to delete that page, and click the pushpin to pin that page permanently into position.

Search tools

Once you know how to use your browser and start surfing, you'll wonder: Among several billion web pages, how do you find the one you want? Use a **search tool,** often referred to as a search engine. You don't have to buy or install search tools—they are just on the web, like any of the other web pages. But they are different from other web pages in that you can type in the names of subjects you want to find, and the search tool will go look for it.

Important Point Number One

When you enter a query in a search tool, it does not go running all over the world looking for pages that match your query. **It looks only in its own database** that it has compiled according to its own special criteria. There are many search tools, and they each have their own criteria. So you might ask three different search tools to find "Briards" (a dog breed) and come up with three different lists of web pages about Briards.

Important Point Number Two

Each search tool has different rules for finding information. **Read their Tips or Help section.** It will tell you critical details about how to enter a query so results can be found. As search tools are improved, their rules change, so when you see a new look on your favorite search page, check the Help section again.

Enter this web address: **google.com.**

Or, no matter which page you're viewing, you can use this field to search in Google!

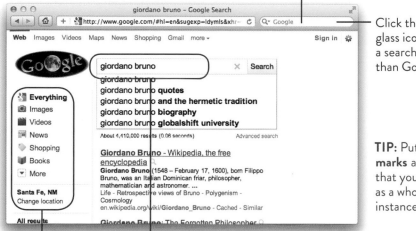

Click the magnifying glass icon to choose a search engine other than Google.

TIP: Put **quotation marks** around words that you want to find as a whole phrase (for instance, "mary sidney").

Select one of these options to narrow your search.

Enter (type) your query in here. You'll notice that Google gives you options as you type. Select any of those options **or** type in your own search request.

Press Return or click the "Search" button. See the results below.

To narrow the search with specific parameters, click here.

Google tells you how many web pages it found that refer to your search term, and shows the search speed.

These are the results of the simple search shown above. **Single-click any link to go to that page.**

If you Command-click a link, the new page will open in a **new tab.** That way you won't lose this page full of results.

Use Reader mode to remove web page clutter

Safari can improve the readability of some web pages by showing only the essential text and graphics. When you see a "Reader" badge on the right side of the address field (circled, below), click it to display the current page as text and graphics only, and hide all of the non-related clutter that's on the page.

Click the Reader button to enter Reader mode. Click the button again to exit Reader mode.

Move the pointer over the bottom edge of the page to reveal pop-up controls to enlarge, reduce, mail, or print the web page (shown at the bottom of the page). To exit the Reader, click the **X** in the pop-up controls, or click the Reader button again.

The original page.

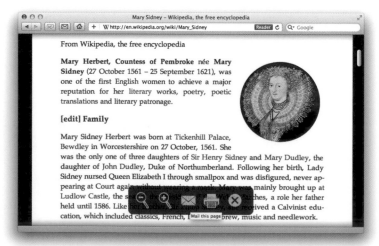

The same page displayed in the Reader mode.

To create a Reading List of web pages to read later, click the Reading List icon (shown on the right) that appears on the left side of the Safari Bookmarks Bar. You must be connected to the Internet to create a Reading List and to retrieve and read the items in the list.

Make a Reading List

To add the current web page to your Reading List, click the "Add Page" button (circled below) in the Reading List sidebar that opens.

Click to hide or show the Reading List sidebar.

To see a list of all bookmarked pages, both read and unread, click the "All" button (shown below).

To narrow the list to only unread bookmarked pages, click the "Unread" button.

To clear an individual item from the list, move the pointer over the item, then click the circled **X** icon that appears in the corner of the item (circled, below).

To clear all items from the list, click the "Clear All" button.

Remember. . . .

- You don't need to type **http://** in a web address.
- Make and use your **bookmarks!**
- Read the **search tips** in Google to learn how to find what you want on the web.
- Take advantage of the **Home** button!

I browse.   Deal with it.

Let's do Email 11

The Mac application for email is called **Mail.** As you'd expect, with Mail you can write email messages, send messages, and receive messages—that's what this chapter covers. Mail actually goes way beyond those basic functions; it has many useful tools for organizing, formatting, searching, and filtering email. But to keep this book "little," I had to put the more detailed information about the other features into *Mac OS X Lion: Peachpit Learning Series.* This chapter in your hands, however, will get you sending and receiving email and attachments, using Notes and To Dos, and creating fancy stationery.

You must have an Internet connection already set up, as explained in Chapter 9, and you must **already have an email account** with someone. Your ISP probably gave you an email account, as also explained in Chapter 9, or you can get a free email address at Gmail.com, Yahoo.com, or Apple.com.

The **Address Book** is a separate application that works in conjunction with Mail. You can save your favorite email addresses, make a group list to send a message to a number of people at once, enter an address in a new message with the click of the mouse, and more.

In this chapter

Let your Mac set up your account 146
Set up your account manually 147
Mail 149
    The Viewer window 149
    Write and send an email message 150
    Use stationery 151
    Check for messages 152
    Tips for writing messages 153
    Tips for replying to messages 154
    Customize the Viewer window 155
    Conversations in your email window . . . 156
    Attach a file a message 158
    Download an attachment
      someone sent you 160
    Create a Note 161

Address Book 162
    Add new names and addresses
      to Address Book 162
    Add a name and address from Mail 164
    Send email to someone
      from your Address Book 165
    Address an email message in Mail
      using the Address Pane 165
Also Try This 166
    Make a group mailing list 166
    Send email to a group mailing list 167
    Have your mail read out loud to you . . . 167
Remember 168

Let your Mac set up your account

Before Mail can check your email account, you must set up your account. *If you entered your email information when you first turned on your Mac, Mail is ready to go and you can* **skip to page 149.**

It's easy to add your email account to Mail if you didn't do it when you first installed Lion or turned on your new Mac, and it's easy to add another account at any time.

To set up a Mail account (or an iChat account, Calendar settings, and/or to transfer your Address Book):

1 Open the "Mail, Contacts & Calendars" preferences: From the Apple menu, choose "System Preferences…," then click the icon shown to the left. You'll see the pane shown below-left.

2 If you have one of the types listed, single-click its name (if not, see below). You'll be asked for your email address and its password and a couple of other questions. If all goes well, your Mac sets up your account and that's it!

3 At any time you can click the account name on the left, then choose to turn on or off the various services.

To set up a POP account (which is just about any other email account besides the services listed above), click **"Other."** Enter your email address and password, and if the Mac can set it up, it will.

But it might tell you that it's not able to do it and pass you off to the manual setup. Make sure you have the information explained on the opposite page, then follow the simple steps on page 148.

You need the information listed below to create an email account. This information comes from your Internet Service Provider (ISP), as explained in Chapter 9, so if you don't know what an ISP is, please read that information!

Set up your account manually

Email address: Your provider gave you an email address, or asked you to create one. It looks something like this:

yourname@isp.com   *or*   yourname@att.net

Incoming mail server: Your provider will tell you exactly what this is. It's usually something like this:

mail.me.com   *or*   pop.earthlink.net

> *Advanced note:* If you have an ISP but you also have several different email accounts from other places, such as from your own domain or someone's web site, ask your host what the incoming mail server is for that account.

Account type: It's usually either a POP account or IMAP. Most local providers are POP, and you won't go wrong by choosing POP if you don't know yet which it is.

User name: This is *usually* the same as your email address, but *not always* because it's actually the user name for your account *with that provider.* Use your email address as your user name, and if it doesn't work, call your provider and ask them what it is.

Password: This is the password for your email account.

Outgoing Mail Server, or SMTP: No matter how many email accounts you have from how many different places, you can always use the SMTP of the provider you pay each month to connect you to the Internet. For instance, I have a dozen different email accounts at a dozen different servers, but I use the same SMTP for every one of them—I use Comcast because that's who I pay each month. All of my email goes out through Comcast. An SMTP address usually looks something like this:

smtp.comcast.net

If you have several accounts on your laptop and you want to send mail when you are away from home, you can setup individual SMTPs for those accounts; ask your provider or check their web site for the SMTP info.

With the above information in hand, follow the steps on the next page.

Add, change, or customize a Mail account

When you open Mail for the first time, it asks for the information as shown below and explained on the previous pages. If you already set up your Mail account when you first turned on your Mac, you can skip to the next page.

You can add more accounts, change existing information, and customize your accounts from the Mail preferences dialog box: Go to the Mail menu, choose "Preferences…," and single-click the Accounts button in the toolbar (shown circled).

To add a new account, single-click the + sign.

If you enter your email password here, you won't have to enter it every time you check your mail. This means, however, that anyone with access to your computer can check your email.

Enter your existing email account name and password.

For information about your "incoming mail server," see page 144.

There are just a couple of windows like this where you will be asked to fill in the information.

Don't worry if you don't know exactly what to enter here—you can always change it in the Mail preferences Accounts pane (as shown above). Feel free to click "Cancel" and fill in the account information later.

The **basic** things you will be doing in **Mail** are checking messages, replying to messages, and composing new messages. On these next few pages are directions for how to do just that. But don't neglect Notes!

Mail

Mail opens up to the **Viewer window.** This window is customizable in so many ways, so if yours doesn't look exactly like this, don't worry. Learn more about the Viewer window on pages 155–157.

If you open Mail and don't see this window, go to the File menu and choose "New Viewer Window."

The Viewer window

Click "New Message" to compose and send a message.

To see text labels under the icons, Command-click (or right-click) in the Toolbar and choose "Icon and Text."

This is the Favorites bar.

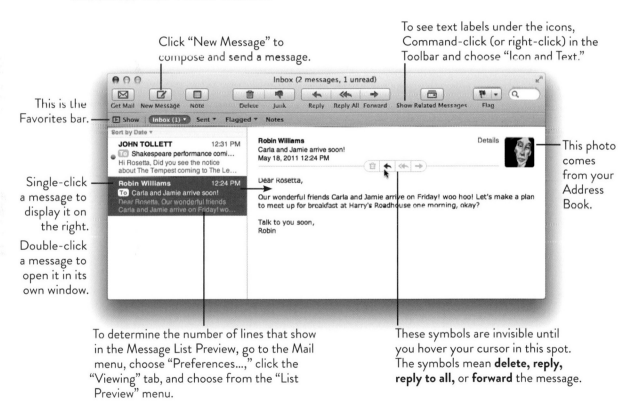

Single-click a message to display it on the right.

Double-click a message to open it in its own window.

This photo comes from your Address Book.

To determine the number of lines that show in the Message List Preview, go to the Mail menu, choose "Preferences…," click the "Viewing" tab, and choose from the "List Preview" menu.

These symbols are invisible until you hover your cursor in this spot. The symbols mean **delete, reply, reply to all,** or **forward** the message.

149

Write and send an email message

If you don't know anyone's email address to write to, you can **write a message** to yourself, send it, and you'll get it within a few minutes.

Exercise 1: Write an email message and send it.

1 Click the "New Message" button in the toolbar to open a "New Message" window, as shown below (except yours will be blank).

An email address must have an @ symbol (at), and there must be a "domain name" with a dot, such as "ratz.com," "aol.com," "earthlink.net," etc.

2 Click in the "To" field and type an email address, as shown above. You can type more than one address in here, as long as you type a comma after each one.

> **Note:** If the person you are sending email to is already in your Address Book (see pages 162–165) or "Previous Recipients" list (in the Window menu in Mail), Mail replaces the email address with that person's name as soon as you type it. If you need to change or edit that name, single-click the name and a little menu pops up; choose the action you want to take (as shown below).

Don't be alarmed if the email address you're typing suddenly changes to a person's name. If you need to make any corrections, single-click the tiny triangle at the end of name and you'll get the menu shown here.

3 To send a copy of this same letter to someone else, click in the "Cc" field and type an address. You can type more than one address, each separated by a comma.

Adding a name to the "Cc" field is really no different from typing more than one address in the "To" field; it's just a subtle statement that the message really belongs to the person in the "To" field, and someone else is getting a copy of it for some reason.

4 Click in the "Subject" field and type a message description. *Be specific*—the recipient needs to know that your message is not junk mail.

5 Click in the blank message area and type your message!

6 Click the "Send" icon in the toolbar. Off it goes.

Your copy of the sent message will be stored in the sidebar in the "Sent" folder.

Use stationery

Apple has created fancy "HTML" stationery for you to use. All you do is open a new message window and click the button to "Show Stationery" (circled below). You'll see a row of stationery icons; click the type of stationery you want, and then just replace the existing fake text with your own.

To add photos, click the "Photo Browser" button (also circled below) to display your photo collection from iPhoto.

Drag photos from the Photo Browser and drop them on the existing photos in the email message. **Or** drag an image from anywhere in your computer and drop it on a photo to replace it. Then just send your fancy message!

Click one of these categories, then click the page you want to use.

Click on the text and type to replace it with your own message.

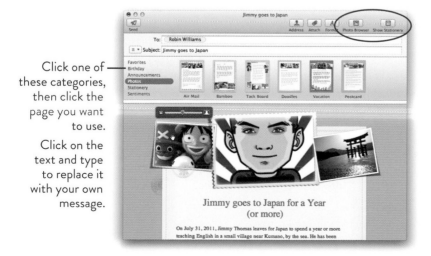

Check for messages

If you have a broadband Internet connection and if you leave the Mail application open all the time, the Mail icon in the Dock will continually tell you how many new messages you have.

When new messages arrive, the Mail icon in the Dock displays how many unread messages you have.

If you have a dial-up connection, the number in the Dock only appears when you are connected and Mail has checked your account for new messages.

Exercise 2: Check for messages.

1 Click once on the Mail icon in the Dock to open Mail (you must be connected to the Internet, of course).

2 Click the "Get Mail" icon in the toolbar.

The "Inbox" button might display a number—if so, that number indicates how many *unread* messages are in your Inbox.

Your messages appear in the Message Preview List that shows the first couple of lines of the message.

3 Single-click a message to display its contents in the Message Pane to the right.

You can also double-click a message preview, and it will open in its own window.

Exercise 3: Reply to the sender of a message.

1 Select the message so its contents appear in the Message Pane.

2 Single-click the "Reply" button in the toolbar.

3 A message window opens that contains the original sender's address in the "To" field, and the original message formatted as a quote (in color and with a line down the left side). Type your reply *above* the quote, then click the "Send" button in the toolbar.

> **TIP:** If you select a portion of the text *before* you click "Reply," just that portion of text will be copied into the new email message!

Here are a few extra tips to keep in mind as you compose new messages.

To save a message as a draft: As soon as you start typing a new message, Mail saves it in the Drafts folder (you can also press Command S to save the very latest version). The message will be saved in the Drafts folder within your Mailboxes sidebar. You will only see the Drafts button when you're writing a new message or if something has been left unfinished.

To open the draft ("restore" it) later for editing: Single-click the "Drafts" button in the toolbar, then double-click the desired draft in the list. It opens and you can continue working.

Format your message: Click the "A" button in the toolbar, which is the *Format* button, to get options for changing the font of your text, its size and color, the alignment, etc. Remember, first select the text, and then apply the formatting. Or make your selections before you start typing, and then everything you type will be in that format (which you can, of course, change).

To send a Bcc (blind courtesy copy):

1 Address and write your message as usual.

2 Press the *Customize* button (circled, below) to get the little menu shown below. Choose "Bcc Address Field." This puts a new field in the address area. Any address(es) you type in this field will *not* be seen by anyone whose address is in the "To" or "Cc" field.

Tips for replying to messages

Here are a few extra tips to keep in mind as you reply to messages that have been sent to you.

To reply to all recipients of a message:

Mail that you receive may have been sent to multiple recipients either directly or as carbon copies (Cc). You can choose to reply to *all* recipients with one email (the reply will not include anyone in the hidden Bcc list; see the next page).

1 If the message is not already open, double-click the message in the Viewer window to open it.

2 In the message window, click the "Reply All" button in the toolbar.

3 Type your reply above the original quoted message, then click the "Send" button in the toolbar.

To forward a message:

A message that you forward is left in your box and a copy is sent to the person of your choice.

1 Double-click a message in the Viewer window.

2 Select the part of the message that you want to forward: Press-and-drag over the specific text. Just the information you select will be forwarded. (If you really want to send the entire message, don't select anything before you go to Step 3.)

3 Click the "Forward" button in the toolbar.

Delete any and everything that is not part of the actual message; delete every email address from the message area!!! Do NOT forward a message full of garbage. Very bad things will happen if you forward meaningless junk or a list of email addresses.

4 Type your comments *above* the original quoted message, then click the "Send" button in the toolbar. It's really nice to add a personal message to anything you forward. And please don't forward stupid stuff—make sure it's worth someone's time to get it and that it's not loaded with a foot of garbage!

The Viewer window can be customized in a number of ways. One of the most useful things you will do is display the Sidebar, as shown below. If you have more than one email account, the Sidebar displays the unread messages for each one. You can make new folders in which to organize messages, and if you make Notes or flag certain messages, they will be organized for you in this Sidebar. **To show the Sidebar,** click the "Show" button; to hide it again, guess what? Click "Hide"!

Customize the Viewer window

The blue orb tells me this is an unread message.

The green orb tells me this person is online and available in iChat.

Hide or show the Sidebar.

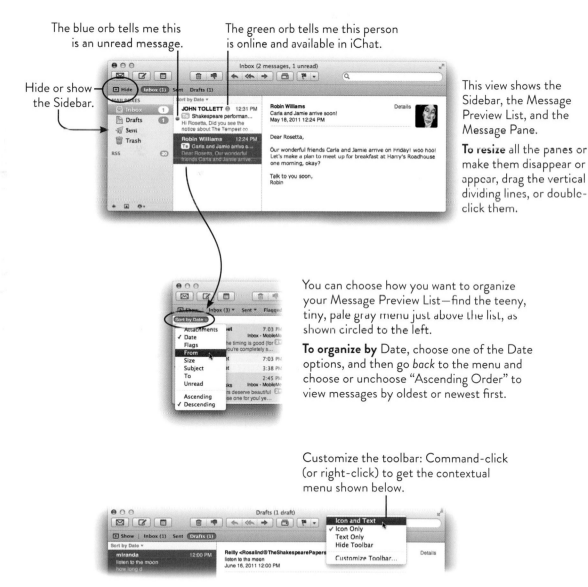

This view shows the Sidebar, the Message Preview List, and the Message Pane.

To resize all the panes or make them disappear or appear, drag the vertical dividing lines, or double-click them.

You can choose how you want to organize your Message Preview List—find the teeny, tiny, pale gray menu just above the list, as shown circled to the left.

To organize by Date, choose one of the Date options, and then go *back* to the menu and choose or unchoose "Ascending Order" to view messages by oldest or newest first.

Customize the toolbar: Command-click (or right-click) to get the contextual menu shown below.

155

Conversations in your email window

Conversations is a feature in which every message regarding a particular subject is grouped together, numbered in order of being received; if a message in another mailbox pertains to this subject, it also appears in the Conversation, but without a number. This can make your Mail window look rather complicated, so you might want to avoid using conversations until you feel comfortable with the basic email process.

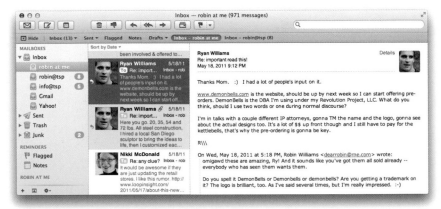

This is a typical Mail layout, with the Sidebar showing your Inboxes, the Message Preview List showing your mail, and the Message Pane showing the email text.

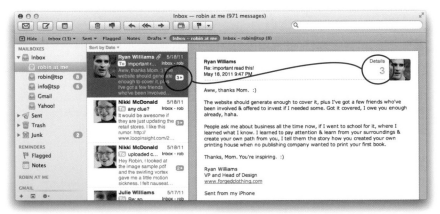

From the View menu, choose "Organize by Conversation." The Message Preview List condenses the related messages and puts the most recent sender at the top with a number in the Message List indicating how many messages are in the Conversation.

All the related messages are in the Message Pane; scroll down to read them. The number in the Message Pane indicates which number message this is in that particular Conversation (also called a *thread*).

Although this looks like *four* messages, the top part is actually the first message in the list beneath.

Once your email is in Conversation view, go to the View menu and choose "Expand All Conversations." The newest email in the thread displays rows of previous messages beneath it, as shown above. Once you select a message, you can use your arrow keys to select other messages in that Conversation.

To view *your* message in the thread, click a curved arrow (circled, above).

Notice the triangle (circled, above) next to the number in the first message now points downward, indicating the Conversation is expanded. Click that number and it will "collapse" the Conversation (or from the View menu, choose "Collapse All Conversations").

Important note: If you delete the top (most recent) message in a Conversation, *every email in that Conversation goes to the Trash!* To save an individual message from the Conversation, you can move an email from a Conversation and drop it into another mailbox; it remains part of the thread, but it won't get deleted along with the others.

Also be sure to check out the **preferences for Conversations:** From the Mail menu, choose "Preferences...." Click the "Viewing" tab. The bottom portion of the pane provides options for you to consider regarding Conversations. For instance, if you prefer not to view messages by Conversations, you could have related message highlighted with a color instead.

Attach a file to a message Sometimes you want to **send someone a photo** you took or a text file that you created in your word processor. You can send it as an attachment, but keep in mind that not everyone can read your attachments. To be able to read a file someone else sends, the other person must have a program that can open that particular type of file.

Sending photographs is pretty easy—digital cameras always create the photographs in the file format called "JPEG" (pronounced *jay peg*), with the three-letter extension at the end of ".jpg." Just about anyone can open a JPEG.

Exercise 4: Attach a file to an email message.

1 Open a new message, address it, and type your message.

It's *polite* to type a message—don't just send a file without any sort of note! If it's something other than a photograph, it can be helpful to state what kind of file it is and how it was created. ("This is a presentation file created in Keynote on a Mac using OS X.")

2 Click the "Attach" button in the message window toolbar, or choose "Attach File..." from the File menu. The standard Open dialog box appears so you can find and select the file you wish to attach.

3 Find the file, select it, then click "Open."

If you don't know how to find files in the Open window, see page 89 (the Open dialog box is similar to the Save As dialog box shown), *or* skip steps 2 and 3 and use the alternate method explained below.

Alternate method of attaching a file:

Either use the Photo Browser, as shown on the opposite page, or simply drag any file from anywhere on your computer and drop it into a message window.

Exercise 5: Remove an attachment from a message you are sending.

■ Select the attachment in the "New Message" window (click it once), then press the Delete key.

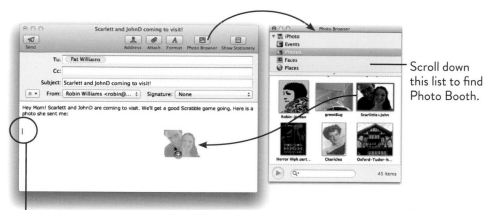

Scroll down this list to find Photo Booth.

The photo will land where the insertion point is flashing (as explained on pages 66–67), so keep your eye on the insertion point!

In a new message, click the "Photo Browser" icon to see all of your photos that you've stored in iPhoto or created in Photo Booth. Just find the photo you want and drag it into the email message.

Or drag a file from anywhere on your Mac and drop it in the email message window.

The original file does not leave with the email—the original stays right where it is and a **copy** is sent with the email.

Here is what the attachment looks like once I drop it into the message.

Depending on the file, you might see the actual image here in the message pane, and the recipient might also see the actual image. She can drag it to her Desktop if she wants to keep it, or save it into a folder, as explained on the next page.

As you choose a visual size from the menu to the right, the file size of the message will change accordingly.

Use this menu to make the file a reasonable size for going through the Internet. Less than 500 KB is good.

159

Download an attachment someone sent you

Mail makes it very easy to **download (copy) files from an email** to your Mac. Now, whether you can actually "open" a file someone sent you, once it's on your Desktop, is a completely different matter! If someone sends you a file created in a program you don't have on your Mac, you might not be able to open it. That's not your fault—the person sending the file should ask if you can open that file type, and if not, prepare the file in such a way that you can. But that's a separate big topic.

Never open attachments from someone you don't know! And never click on a link in an email message if you don't know who the message is from *or* if there is no personal message from that person included with the link.

Exercise 6: Download an attachment someone sent you in an email message.

- Open the email that contains the attachment. Then do *one* of these things:

    Either drag the file from the email and drop it on your Desktop. You might get a message that says you can't get the file until it has been downloaded; if you do, just click the button to download the file, and then you will be able to drag it off.

    Or Control-click (or right-click) on the image to get the contextual menu, as shown below. Choose an option.

If an attached file has an underline, you can just click it to open the file.

The **Notes** feature in Mail is a handy place to store ideas, thoughts, or any other information you want to keep track of.

Exercise 7: Create a new Note.

1 Click the "Note" button in Mail's toolbar. (This button is only available when you're in the main viewer window, *not when an email message is open and active.*)

2 A "New Note" window opens in which you can type a brief or lengthy note, or paste in text that you copied from an email message or anywhere else. Mail uses your first line of text as the subject of the note and shows the first line in Mail's list of Notes (keep that in mind as you write your note).

Use the toolbar buttons to format your text, add an attachment, or email the Note in a message.

3 To create an automatically bulleted or numbered list, go to the Format menu at the top of your screen, slide down to "Lists," and choose the type of list you want. Type your list, hitting a Return after each item. To stop the list so you can type regular text, hit the Return key twice.

4 When finished, click "Done."

As soon as you make your first Note (or select a message and click the Flag icon to flag it), a new "Reminders" section appears in the Sidebar, as shown below. Click "Notes" to display all of them in their own viewer window. You'll also see the Notes appear in your list of email messages when viewing an Inbox.

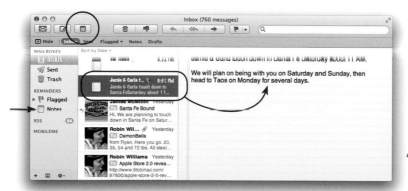

Create a Note

Notes you make on your iPhone appear in Mail and vice versa.

TIP: The default font for Notes is practically unreadable. You can change it:

Go to the Mail menu and choose "Preferences…."

Click the icon in the toolbar, "Fonts & Colors."

To the right of the field for "Note font," click the button "Select…" and choose a font and size.

Select a Note in the Message Preview List.

Or to show *only* Notes in the Message Preview List, click the "Notes" item in the Sidebar.

161

Address Book

The Address Book icon
is in your Dock,
the Applications folder,
and Launchpad.

The **Address Book** works independently as well as in conjunction with Mail to create Address Cards that store contact information for individuals and groups. When Mail is open, you can automatically create an Address Book entry for anyone who sent mail to you. When you open the Address Book from a new message you're writing, you can automatically address email to an individual or an entire group.

Search for information on any card; simply enter text in this search field.

If your Address Book opens to this view, click the red bookmark at the top, *or* double-click a name, *or* click "All Contacts."

To add a new name and card, click this + sign.

Click to **edit** the selected card; click again when finished.

Add new names and addresses to Address Book

You can **add a new address card** to the Address Book from either the Address Book (explained below) or Mail (see page 164).

Exercise 1: Add a new address card while using Address Book.

1 Open the Address Book, if it isn't already.

2 Single-click the **+** at the bottom of the left page.

3 This makes a new card automatically appear and the "First" field is already selected for you, waiting for you to type the person's first name.

4 Type the person's first name, then hit the Tab key, which will automatically select the "Last" field.

   Type the last name, then hit Tab, etc. Continue to fill in all the information you know.

5 If a label is changeable, you'll see a tiny arrow. For instance, maybe you want to change the label "mobile" to "cell." Single-click the tiny arrow and you'll get a little pop-up menu, as shown below. Choose one of the pre-named labels, *or* choose "Custom…" and type in the name of the label you want.

6 Click the red – sign to delete the label and field to its right, but keep in mind that any field that has no information will not appear on the actual card anyway.

7 When you're finished, click the "Edit" button at the bottom of the card.

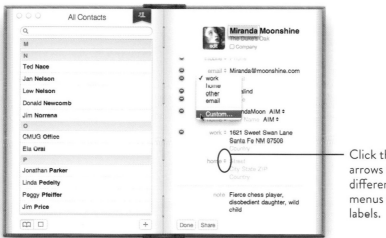

Click the tiny arrows to get different pop-up menus for different labels.

Exercise 1a: Add an image to the address card.

1 Double-click the image space (you don't have to click the Edit button first).

2 Do one of the following to add a photo:

Drag an image from iPhoto or from your Desktop and drop it into the photo "well" that appears.

Click "Choose…" to select an image from anywhere on your hard disk.

Click the camera icon to take a photo.

3 If you like, click the *Effects* button to add an effect.

4 Click "Set" to put the image on the card.

Once you add an image, it will appear in an iChat session with this person, and it will appear in any email she sends you. Contacts and photos you add to your iPhone will appear in Address Book when you sync via iTunes.

Add a name and address from Mail

You can add anyone's address to your Address Book as soon as she sends you an email.

Exercise 2: Add a sender's email address to your Address Book instantly.

1 Open the **Mail** program.

2 Either single-click an email in your list to select it, *or* double-click to open the message.

3 From the "Message" menu in the menu bar across the top of your screen, choose "Add Sender To Address Book," *or* press Command Shift Y. The Address Book will not open, but the sender's address will be added.

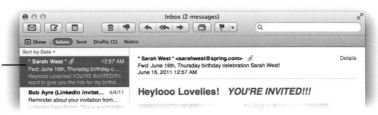

Single-click to select a sender's email in your list, then press Command Shift Y.

Check on that address later, though, because if a person's first and last names are not included in her own email address, you'll find the new address in your Address Book at the very top of the "Name" column as <No Name>. **Edit** that card to add the person's name so she is sorted in the list properly.

From your Address Book, you can **address an email message.** This assumes, of course, that you have this person's email address in your Address Book.

Send email to someone from your Address Book

Exercise 3: Use your Address Book to send someone an email.

1 Open your Address Book and select the person to whom you want to send email (single-click his name).

2 Single-click the tiny label that's to the *left* of the email address. A menu pops up, as shown below.

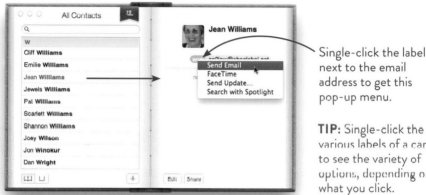

Single-click the label next to the email address to get this pop-up menu.

TIP: Single-click the various labels of a card to see the variety of options, depending on what you click.

3 Choose "Send Email," and a new message window appears with that person's address in the "To" field.

If you're in Mail, you don't have to get your Address Book to address a message.

Address an email message in Mail using the Address Pane

Exercise 4: Address a message from the Address Pane.

1 **In Mail,** single-click the "Address" icon in the toolbar.

If the Address icon is not in the toolbar, Control-click (or right-click) on the toolbar and choose "Customize Toolbar...." Drag the icon to the toolbar, then click "Done."

2 A limited version of the Address Book opens, as shown below. You can't add or delete addresses in this pane, but you can select any number of addresses or groups (Command-click to select more than one), then click the "To" button. A new message appears already addressed.

Also Try This

Make a group mailing list

If you regularly send email to a specific group of people, you can make a **group list in your Address Book** so that with one click of the button, your email will be sent to everyone on the list.

PLEASE don't stick everyone in your whole dang Address Book in a group list!!! Not everyone wants you to forward every joke and every virus warning (which Macs don't get anyway)!

Create groups that have specific purposes. You might want one group list just for family members, another for your poker club, one you send your travelogues to, and one for those people who have called you up and said, "Please put me on your mailing list for every stupid joke that runs across the Internet!" The same name can be in many different groups.

It's easy to make a group list, and it's easy to send a message to one or more groups at once.

To make a group list:

1 If you see the red bookmark on the left page with two heads on it, click it (if you see a single-headed bookmark on the right page, stay there).

2 Click the plus sign (**+**) at the bottom of the left page.

3 In the field for the new group that appears, type the name of your group. Hit Return or Enter.

4 Single-click the "All Contacts" group on that page.

5 Drag names from the list on the right-hand page and drop them into the new group.

You can put the same name in any number of groups; all names will always be in the "All Contacts" list.

To return to the main page of contacts, single-click the red bookmark on the right-hand page.

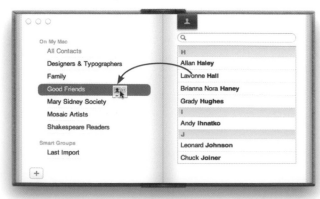

To send email to a group list:

■ Simply type the name of the group in the "To" field.

Send email
to a group mailing list

To make sure the recipients do not see the entire list of email addresses:

1 In **Mail,** go to the Mail preferences (in the Mail menu).

2 Click the "Composing" icon in the toolbar.

3 Make sure there is **no** checkmark in the option "When sending to a group, show all member addresses."

This is the polite thing to do. All of us get too much mail, and it's not a good idea to give everyone on your list the actual addresses of everyone else.

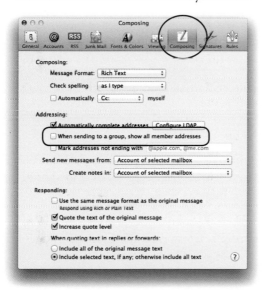

Have your mail read out loud to you:

1 Open an email message.

2 Press-and-drag over the text that you want to have read aloud, *or* hit Command A to select all.

3 From the Edit menu, slide down to "Speech," then choose "Start Speaking."

You can go work on anything else you like on your Mac, and your mail will be read to you.

4 To stop the voice, repeat step 3 and choose "Stop Speaking."

Have your mail read
out loud to you

Remember. . .

- Do not type an email in **ALL CAPS.** Since we can't hear voices in an email, all caps is the visual equivalent of shouting. And it's just as annoying in print as it is in person.

- It's very easy to make a group mailing list. But don't send email to a list of people unless you *know* everyone on that list *wants* to receive that mail. **Ask first** before putting someone on your list, please!

- When you **forward a message** to someone, please take a few seconds to get rid of all the superfluous garbage that ends up in a forwarded message. The easy way to do this is to select just the actual lines you want to forward *before* you click the Forward button.

- You can have your **email read out loud** to you with the click of a button! See page 167.

Other Useful
Features   12

Well, if you've worked through all of the exercises in this "little" book, you should be pretty comfortable with your Mac by now. This chapter introduces you to a couple of other features that you might like to know as you spend more time with your computer.

Good luck! *Now go forward—in all directions!*

In this chapter

System Preferences. 170
    Desktop & Screen Saver. 171
Aliases 172
    Make an alias .172
    Details of aliases. 173
Search for files on your Mac with Spotlight. .174
    Narrow the search 176
    Find types of files. 176
    Spotlight in applications 177
Stickies. 178
Sleep, Restart, Shut Down, or Log Out 179
Burn a CD or DVD with a Burn Folder 180
AirDrop 181
Mission Control 182
Spaces 184
Exposé 186
Dashboard: Widgets at your fingertips 187
Remember. 188

System Preferences

The System Preferences allow you to change the settings of a number of features on your computer. This will become a familiar process to you as you work with your Mac. In this little book, all I can do is point you to the System Preferences and suggest you check them out. Most of them are very self-explanatory.

This is the System Preferences icon that is usually in your Dock.

To open System Preferences:

- The icon shown to the left should be in your Dock. Single-click it.

    Or from the Apple menu, choose "System Preferences… ."

Use this search field to find the appropriate pane. For instance, if you accidentally turned on VoiceOver when you set up your Mac, find which preference pane will turn it off: Type "voiceover" in this field.

To turn on scroll bars, use the General preferences; choose "Always."

To turn on your right mouse button (the secondary button), use the Mouse preferences.

Exercise: Explore the System Preferences.

1 **To open a preference pane,** single-click any icon. The new pane will **replace** the one you see. For now, click the first icon, "Appearance."

2 Explore the options in this pane.

3 **To go back to the main pane,** single-click the "Show All" button in the upper left of the window, or press Command L.

4 Check out the options in each pane. When you're finished, just click the red button to close.

This is an example of the kind of thing System Preferences can do for you: The **Desktop & Screen Saver** preferences pane lets you customize the appearance of your Desktop and provides some amazing options for screen savers (which are animated graphics that appear on your screen when you're not using your Mac).

**Desktop
& Screen Saver**

Desktop &
Screen Saver

Exercise: Change your Desktop background.

1 In System Preferences, click "Desktop & Screen Saver."

2 Click the **Desktop** tab (circled below) to display the Desktop panel.

3 Select a folder in the left-hand list; its contents are shown in the panel on the right.

4 Select an image on the right (single-click it), and it immediately appears in the thumbnail space in the top portion of the pane, as well as on the Desktop.

 You can also use any photo or graphic image that's in iPhoto or your Pictures folder: Choose "iPhoto" or "Folders" from the list shown below to select one of your own photos.

5 When you've decided on a Desktop image, click the red Close button to close the preferences.

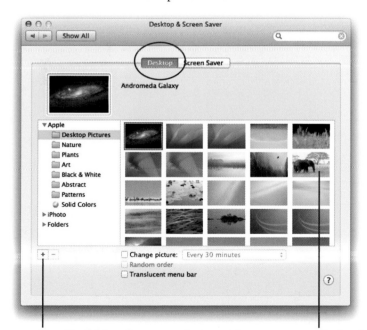

To add a folder of your own that contains images, click the + button and choose a folder from the dialog box that appears. It will be placed inside the "Folders" folder.

Single-click any image to turn it into the background on your monitor.

Aliases

Methinks I scent the morning air

An alias looks just like the original icon, but there's a small arrow in the bottom-left corner.

An **alias** is an "empty" icon that represents the real thing. You create aliases so you don't have to go find the original file every time you want to use it—you can put aliases where they are easier to find, and then keep the originals in their important folders.

You can make aliases of applications, documents, folders, utilities, games, etc. Aliases are wonderful tools for organizing your work—anything you want to use is only one double-click away from wherever you are. Remember, an alias is just a picture that goes and gets the real file.

Make an alias

Exercise: Make an alias.

1 Select the item you want to make an alias of (single-click it).

2 Then choose one of these four ways to make an alias:

   From the File menu, choose "Make Alias."

   Or press Command L.

   Or hold down the Control key and single-click the item. A contextual menu pops up, as shown below; choose "Make Alias."

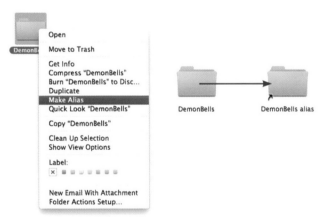

   Or hold down Command Option and drag the file— if you drag it to a different folder or to the Desktop, when you let go you'll have an alias with the word "alias" removed from its name; if you drag to somewhere else in the same folder, you'll have an alias with the word "alias" at the end of it.

Drag the alias icon to wherever you want to keep it. Rename it if you like. The new file does not have to have the word "alias" in its name. And it doesn't matter if you move the original file—the alias can always find it.

Making aliases is easy, but here are some **details** you should understand.

- An alias isn't a *duplicate* of anything; it's just a **pointer** to the real thing. If you double-click an *alias* of Quicken, for instance, it will open your *original* Quicken application, even if the original Quicken is stored in a completely different folder.

- If you **delete** an alias, you don't delete the original— the original is still stored on your hard disk. So you can keep revising your filing system as your needs change. Don't want that alias of Budget Charts cluttering up your Project Plans folder anymore? Fine; throw it away. The original Budget Charts is still where you stored it.

- If you put an item into an *alias* of a **folder,** the item actually gets put into the *original* folder.

- You can **move** an alias and even **rename** an alias. The Mac will still be able to find the original and open it whenever you double-click the alias.

- Even if you move or rename the **original** file, the alias can still find it.

- If you **delete** the **original** file, the Mac does *not* automatically delete any of the aliases you created for that file. When you double-click an alias whose original has been trashed, you will get a message telling you the original could not be located.

Note: Items in the Dock, the Sidebar, or a Finder window Toolbar are already aliases.

Search for files on your Mac with Spotlight

No matter how well organized you keep your Mac, one day it's going to be difficult to **find a particular file.** Perhaps you misplaced it or you copied it from somewhere and can't find it or you don't even know where it went in the first place. **Spotlight** can find anything and everything for you. It finds the text you're looking for whether it's in the name of the file, inside an email message, a PDF, or in the text of a document.

Tips for searching: It doesn't matter whether you type capital or lower case letters—the search will find "Love Letter" even if you search for "love letter."

Spaces, however, do matter. That is, "love letter" will not find "loveletter."

If you don't know the exact name of the file, just type any part of it that you think is in the file name, such as "love."

Exercise: Do a quick and easy search.

1 Open any Finder window.

2 Type part of the name of the file you're looking for into the search field (shown below). As soon as you start typing, the search begins and items appear in a list in the Finder window, as shown on the opposite page.

As you continue typing, the search narrows to match the word or phrase you've typed, and the list of found items changes as you type.

This window is in List View.   This is the search field.

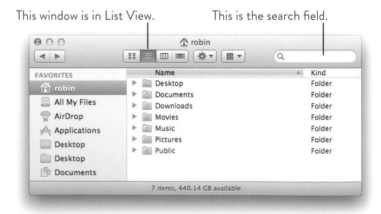

74

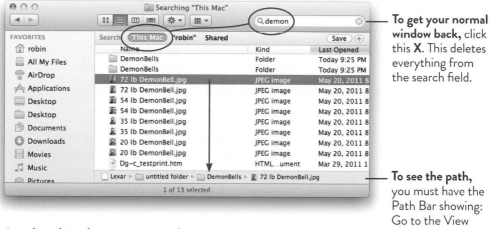

To get your normal window back, click this **X**. This deletes everything from the search field.

To see the path, you must have the Path Bar showing: Go to the View menu to show it.

3 Another thing happens as you begin to type: A search bar appears with locations in which to search. In the example above, you can see it is currently searching "This Mac." Click any other option you see in that tab to search that specific area.

To search only in a specific folder, first select that folder *before* you begin the search process.

4 **To display the *location* of a selected file,** single-click one of the found items in the list to select it; the location is shown in the bottom section of the Finder window, as you can see above.

To open the selected file, double-click it.

To open the window in which the selected file is stored, press Command R.

5 **To get information** about a particular file, single-click a file and press Command I to get the Info window, as shown to the right.

— *continued*

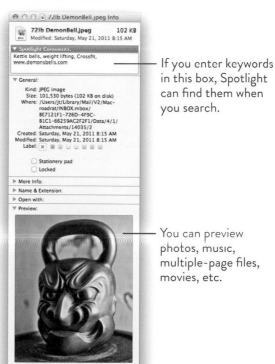

If you enter keywords in this box, Spotlight can find them when you search.

You can preview photos, music, multiple-page files, movies, etc.

175

Narrow the search   You can get even more specific with a search. Follow the steps on the previous pages. Plus:

- Click the **+** button to add a parameter. Each time you click a **+** button, you'll add another parameter.

  Of course, click a **–** button to delete a parameter.

- Each parameter can be changed: Single-click it and choose something else, if you like.

  Each parameter has specific options you can change: Single-click the menu to its right and choose the options. You'll see different options for each parameter. Some will display fields in which you can enter information. The best way to learn how to use it is to experiment!

Find types of files   Leave the search field blank and use just the parameters (as explained above) to find files. For instance, you can find every "Image" you have opened "Since Yesterday" or as shown below, I found every JPEG with the word "demon" in the title that I have stored on this Mac.

If you *do* add a search term in the field, you can limit the search even further—you might want to find every "Image" you opened "Since Yesterday" that has the word "heart" involved.

In this example, I set the parameters to find every image that includes the word "demon" in the file.

The search in every application or window on the Mac is powered by a built-in application called Spotlight.

Exercise: Do a quick and easy search.

1 In **Address Book,** select a person's card.

2 Hold down the Control key and click the name; you'll get a contextual menu in which you can choose to Spotlight that person, as shown below. Every email to or from that person or in which that person is mentioned will be found, plus every relevant file on your Mac.

In **Safari, TextEdit, Preview,** or in any **Mail** message, Control-click to get a menu that includes an option to "Search in Spotlight." Experiment in other applications!

Stickies

The **Stickies** application lets you put little Stickie notes all over your screen, just like you'd stick them around the edge of your monitor (my kids tell me my monitor looks like a giant daisy). **The Stickies application is inside your Applications folder.**

This is a tool tip that describes the rolled-up Stickie note above.

Notice above that you can see examples of these features:

- **Change fonts, size, color,** etc., just as in any other Mac application, using the Font panel (press Command T).

- Double-click the title bar of any Stickie note to "roll it up" so **just the title bar shows,** as you can see above ("Board of Directors Meeting"). The first line of type in the note appears in the title bar. Double-click the title bar again to unroll the note.

- Mouse over any note to display a **tool tip** that gives you information about the note, as shown above.

- Drag a **graphic** image from anywhere on your Mac and drop it into the Stickie note.

- A note can hold many pages of text and graphics. You won't see **scroll** bars, but you still scroll, or you can drag the mouse through the text and it will scroll. Resize a Stickie note just as you would any other window—drag the bottom-right corner.

- Notice the red dots under the name "Brianna." This is a visual clue that the **spell checker** is on and working.

To print a Stickie note:

- Click the note you want to print. Then go to the File menu and choose "Print...."

In the Apple menu, the last four options are **Sleep, Restart, Shut Down,** and **Log Out.** Here is a brief description of when you might use each of these options.

- **Sleep** does two things: 1) It turns off the monitor display so your screen goes black, which is especially good for flat panels, and 2) it stops the hard disk from spinning. Both of these features save energy. If your machine goes to sleep, tap any of the keys on your keyboard to make it wake up again.

- **Restart** shuts down your Mac and starts it up again without ever turning off the power. This is easier on the computer than turning off the power and rebooting (turning it back on). You often have to restart after installing new software (or anytime things just start acting weird).

- On **Shut Down,** the Mac takes care of internal business, cleans up everything, and turns itself off (it actually turns off the power).

- You rarely have to Shut Down in Mac OS X—you can leave your machine on for weeks at a time, setting it to sleep automatically after a certain number of idle minutes.

- Use **Log Out** when your Mac has multiple users enabled, and you want to disable one of the user sessions. If you are the only user, you can use it as a safety precaution when you are going to be away from your computer for a while. Log Out brings up a "Log in" screen where you must type your administrator password to get back to your Desktop. (The administrator password is the one that you set up the first time you turned on your Mac. Don't lose that password!!)

Sleep, Restart, Shut Down, or Log Out

I can't cover multiple users in this small book; you'll use the Users & Groups pane in the System Preferences, and if you need help, please see the more advanced book, **Mac OS X Lion: Peachpit Learning Series.**

Burn a CD or DVD with a Burn Folder

This section explains how to burn **data** CDs and DVDs.

To burn **music CDs,** use iTunes: First create a Playlist in iTunes, then insert a blank CD-R, and burn the Playlist to the CD-R.

You'll want to create backups of your important work so you'll be sure to have it in case anything happens to your computer. One way to make a backup is to **burn a CD or DVD.**

The steps below describe how to burn "data files" (as opposed to music or movies) onto a disc.

The **Burn Folder** is the easiest way to burn a CD or DVD. You'll drag items into this special folder, and when you're ready, burn the contents to a disc. Your Mac automatically creates **aliases** of those files (see pages 172–173 for details on aliases). This means that after you burn the disc, you can throw away the entire Burn Folder without destroying any original files.

The wonderful thing about using a Burn Folder is that you can collect items you want to burn without having to actually burn the disc at that moment—you can collect files over the course of a project and when finished, you have a folder ready to back up onto a disc.

Exercise: Create a Burn Folder, put files inside, and burn it.

1 Open a Finder window. Select the window in which you want the Burn Folder to appear. For instance, single-click your Home icon in the Sidebar, *or* single-click the Documents folder icon. *Or* click the Desktop, if you want the folder to appear there. (You can always move the Burn Folder to wherever you like, of course.)

2 From the File menu, choose "New Burn Folder."

3 A folder with the "Burn" icon on it appears in the selected window (shown on the left).

Burn Folder.fpbf

4 **To put a file in the folder** so you can burn it later, just drag and drop files into the Burn Folder. Your Mac will put an *alias* of the file into the Burn Folder, and the original will stay right where it was, safe and sound.

5 **To burn the folder onto a CD or DVD,** first insert a blank CD-R or DVD.

6 **Then** double-click the Burn Folder; a bar across the top of the window appears with a "Burn" button, as shown below. Click the "Burn" button in the window.

If you have a new Mac running Lion and you're in a Wi-Fi area, you'll see "AirDrop" in your Finder window Sidebar. This makes it extremely easy to send files back and forth over any local wireless connection, as in a coffee shop, tea house, office building, or anywhere.

AirDrop

Just click "AirDrop" in your Sidebar (which you've probably done by now). When anyone else on the same network opens his Air-Drop window while you're looking at your AirDrop window, you will all appear in the window together. Just drop a file on someone else's icon. He will be asked if he is willing to receive it, and then to "Save" or "Save and Open" the file. If you save the file, it immediately downloads into your Downloads folder.

John and I both clicked on "AirDrop" in our Sidebars on our laptops.

On my laptop, I'm dropping a file on John's handsome face.

On John's laptop, he has to approve the file transmission.

Mission Control

Mission Control *combines* **Exposé** (a way of showing all open windows at once), **Spaces** (multiple, alternative Desktops), **Dashboard** (a special screen full of small, specialized apps called widgets), and **full-screen apps** (applications that are in full screen viewing mode).

If your screen becomes cluttered with open documents, applications, and windows, **Mission Control** can display every application and window running on your Mac in a single organized screen view so you can select the item you want (shown below).

These are individual *Spaces*. Single-click a Space to bring it forward.

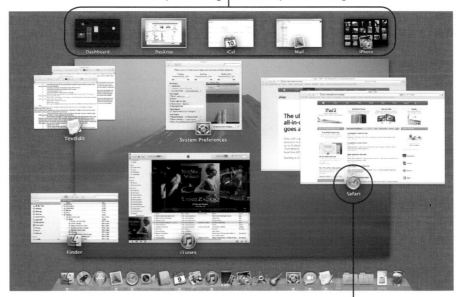

The Mission Control screen.
Click any window in the center part
of the screen to bring it forward.

Icons identify the applications
that are open and running in
the selected Space.

Mission Control shows the applications and their windows that are open. The center area of the screen shows the open windows of the *selected* Space. You can assign up to sixteen alternate "Desktop" Spaces, plus full-screen applications occupy additional Spaces. See the following pages for more about Spaces.

While in Mission Control, click any item or Space that you want to work with to bring it forward as the active item.

The currently active Space is highlighted with a border.

Dashboard has its own Space, assigned by Apple.

In the example above: Dashboard is a Space, the Desktop is a Space, and each of the three apps that are open in full-screen occupies a Space of its own, for a total of five Spaces (at this moment) that are functional. The Space that is highlighted with a border is the one that is currently active and displayed in the center of the Mission Control screen.

Spaces and Mission Control are intricately interwoven, so don't worry if it's confusing at this point. You'll find it's worth the effort to learn how to control it.

To enter Mission Control, do one of the following:

- Press the F9 key (the default keyboard shortcut to show "All Windows").

- You may have to add the fn key (thus, press fn F9), depending on your setting in the Keyboard panel of System Preferences (see page 170).

- You can change the F9 shortcut in the "Mission Control" preferences, shown on the next page.

 - Press the Mission Control key (F3) on your keyboard, if you have one. You may have to add the fn key, as explained above.

- Use *gestures,* if you have a trackpad or mouse that supports Multi-Touch gestures (combinations of finger touches and swipes to scroll, flip through web pages, navigate pages or windows, and more):

- Magic Mouse: Double-tap with two fingers on the surface.

- Multi-Touch trackpad: Swipe upward with three fingers.

To exit Mission Control, do one of the following:

- Click any item in Mission Control.

- Press F9 again (or fn F9 on a laptop).

- Magic Mouse: Double-tap with two fingers on the surface.

- Multi-Touch trackpad: Swipe downward with three fingers.

Spaces

Spaces, incorporated as a part of **Mission Control,** is a convenient way to manage a variety of projects or just plain ol' screen clutter. The idea is to create alternate Desktops, called **Spaces,** then put certain documents or applications in their own Spaces. When you want to work with an application, switch to its custom Space.

There is always at least one Desktop Space, your default Desktop that you always see. When an application is put in full-screen mode, it automatically goes in a new Space of its own. Dashboard has been assigned its own Space. In addition to these Spaces, you can create more.

First, take a quick look at the Mission Control preferences (click the System Preferences icon in the Dock or Launchpad, then click "Mission Control"). The preferences panel has an important option that affects how you interact with Spaces.

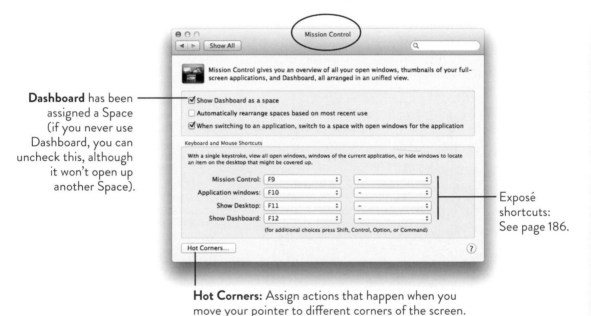

Dashboard has been assigned a Space (if you never use Dashboard, you can uncheck this, although it won't open up another Space).

Exposé shortcuts: See page 186.

Hot Corners: Assign actions that happen when you move your pointer to different corners of the screen.

To create a new Space, do one of the following:

- Open an application, then put it in full-screen mode (click the full-screen mode button, usually in the top-right corner of the window).

 To get out of full-screen mode, shove the pointer into the top of the screen to make the menu bar appear; click the blue arrow icon in the upper-right corner.

- Enter Mission Control (see page 183), then hover your pointer over the top-right corner of the Mission Control screen. The *Add Spaces* button slides out from the corner (shown below); click it.

- Enter Mission Control. Drag an item from the center section of the screen up to the top section, above the large Desktop background image. As you drag, the item becomes smaller and smaller (simulated below). Drop the item on or near the *Add Spaces* button that slides out from the top-right corner. A new Space is created for the item.

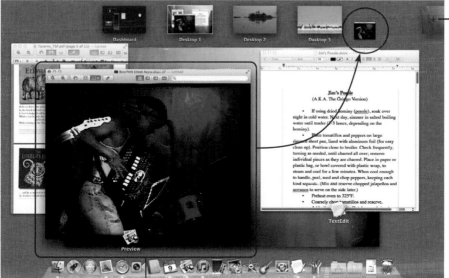

Add Space button.

Drag an item from the center section of Mission Control to the Spaces section at the top of the screen to create a new Space for that item.

To remove a Space, hover your pointer over a Space in Mission Control until a circle-**X** button appears in the top left corner (shown on the right). Click the **X** button.

Exposé

Exposé is an easy way to deal with a lot of open files and applications. It temporarily shows (or hides) open items so you can find what you need. This is how it works:

Let's say you've been working in TextEdit for several days and have created lots of documents. Some are open on your screen, others you have saved into their appropriate folders. Tap the F10 key to show **Application windows.** All open TextEdit files display in the top part of the screen, while *Recent* (and thus closed) TextEdit files and those that have been minimized to the Dock appear as a row of thumbnails. Single-click any document to open it.

Exposé keyboard shortcut **F10**: Show all the open or recent document windows from a specific application.

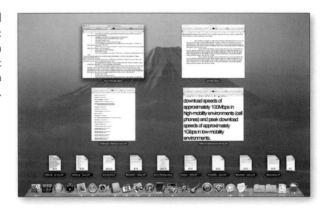

Sometimes you want to **get right to the Desktop/Finder.** Tap the **F11** key: All open windows temporarily move into the margins of the screen—all you can see are wee little edges. Tap F11 again to return the screen to normal. Try it. (If it doesn't work, hold down the fn key and tap F11.)

A cluttered Desktop.

Exposé keyboard shortcut F11: Show the Desktop. The white arrows show the edges of open windows that have been moved out of the way.

Dashboard: Widgets at your fingertips

Dashboard provides quick access to information customized just for you, by you, displayed in the form of **widgets.** The widgets pop up in front of you with the click of a button and disappear just as quickly with another click of a button. You can see what time it is in cities around the world, check the weather in the town where your mother lives, access a dictionary and thesaurus, track the flights of planes, use a calculator, and much more.

Below you see an example of Dashboard with selected widgets showing, plus the **Widget Bar** along the bottom. The widgets appear on top of whatever's on your screen so you don't have to move anything out of the way.

To make Dashboard appear or disappear, tap the F12 key (it's above the Delete key on your keyboard; on a laptop, press fn F12). Or click the Dashboard icon in the Dock (shown, right).

To make the Widget Bar appear or disappear, single-click the **+** sign in the bottom-left corner of your screen. As you can see below, once you show the Widget Bar, the **+** sign becomes an **X**; click the **X** to hide the Widget Bar.

 This is the Dashboard icon.

To customize a Widget's settings, hover the pointer over the Widget, then click the small "i" that appears.

To hide or show this Widget Bar, click this button. When the bar is not visible, this button is a **+** sign.

Click a Widget in the Widget Bar to open it.

To close a Widget, click the **X** in its top-left corner. If the Widget Bar is closed, the **X** isn't visible, but you can press the Option key and the **X** will appear on Widgets you hover the pointer over.

Exit Dashboard.

To see more widgets in this bar, click this button.

187

Remember . . .

- Make an **alias** if you find that you are constantly digging into a particular folder to find a particular file. Or make an alias of the entire folder and put the folder alias right on your Desktop.

- Use the **System Preferences** to customize just about everything on your Mac.

- You can **burn** data files (text, photographs, etc.) to a CD using the method described in this chapter, but to burn music CDs that you can listen to in any player, use iTunes to create a playlist and burn the playlist to a CD. (Directions for using iTunes are in the *Mac OS X Lion: Peachpit Learning Series* book because they wouldn't fit in this book!)

A

About This Mac, 108

accent marks
    charts of, 202–203
    how to type them, 82–83
    special characters, 201

active window, what is it? 38

Address Book, 162–167
    add new names and cards, 162–163
    group mailing list, make and use, 166–167
    search for contact info, 177
    send email from contact page, 165
    transfer Address Book info, 146

AirDrop, 181

aliases, 172–173

All My Files
    displays your files, 5
    window is in an "arranged" icon view, 38, 41

AOL, set up account in Mail, 146

Apple key, 6

Apple menu
    where is it? 3
    Dock options in, 33, 34
    Sleep, Restart, Shut Down, Log Out, 179
        quits applications, 114

Application menu, where is it? 3

applications
    what are they? 64
    active, how to tell, 111
    analogy of typewriter, 108
    Applications folder, 16
    application windows
        document windows in apps, 84
        show and hide all on Desktop, 186
    contextual menu for, 57
    Dock, put an app icon in the Dock, 32
    force an application to quit, 25, 35
    full-screen apps are in their own Spaces,
        182–187
    quit, how to, 112
    show all open windows for that app, 53

arrow keys
    where are they? 6
    keyboard symbols for, 58

arrows in dialog boxes, 60, 61

B

Backspace key is the Delete key, 68

backup data onto a CD or DVD, 180

Baykal, Çaner, 90–91

bit, 108

broadband, 120–121

browser. *See* **Safari.**

burn a CD or DVD, 180

Burn Folder, 180

byte, 108

C

calendar software, iCal, 28
Caps Lock key
    where is it? 6
    everything types in ALL CAPS, 7
CD, DVD
    burn a disk, 180
    open to see what is on the disk, 19
center-aligned text, 75
Chicago Manual of Style, 71
choose a command from a menu, 52–53
click-and-drag, 22
Clipboard
    how it works, 76, 78–79
    Delete versus Cut and the Clipboard, 82
close a document
    how to, 110
    quit vs. close, 108, 110
clutter on your Desktop, manage it
        with Mission Control, 182–188
color-code your files with labels, 62
color wells, how to choose colors, 61
Column View in Finder windows, 42–43
Command key
    where and what is it? 6
    Command-click, how to, 25
        Command-Option-drag, 25
    keyboard symbol for, 58
contextual menus
    examples of, 57
    spell checking with, 69
    two-button mouse is handy, 57
Control-click
    how to, 25
    contextual menus, examples of, 57
Control key
    what and where is it? 6
    keyboard symbol for, 58
Conversations in Mail, 156–157
copyright symbol, how to type it, 201
copy text or a graphic, 76, 81
    keyboard shortcut, 82
    paste what you copied, 79

Cover Flow View, 44
    in Safari bookmarks, 139
cut text or a graphic
    what and how to do it, 76–77
    cut and paste process, example of, 80
    keyboard shortcut, 82
    paste what you cut, 79
    undo the cut, 77

D

Dashboard
    how to use it, 187
    occupies its own Space, 183, 184
default, what is it? 60–61
degree symbol, how to type one, 201
delete files, 115
Delete key
    is also considered the Backspace key, 68
    is different from Cut or Clear, 82
    symbol for, 58
DemonBells.com, 133, 156–157, 175–176
deselect an icon, 15
Desktop
    what is it? 2
    change background image, 171
    Desktop folder in Favorites, 5
    Finder runs the Desktop, 2
    reposition the Dock, 34
    wallpaper, change background image, 171
dialog boxes
    ellipsis indicates you'll get one, 56
    triangles to show or hide information, 60
dial-up phone modem, 121
disclosure buttons or triangles, 60, 61
disks
    burn a CD or DVD for backup, 180
    open a disk to see what's on it, 19
Dock, 27–36
    where is it? 2
    add an item to the Dock, 32
    blue lights in Dock, 30
        if they're missing, how to turn them on, 111
    dividing line in, 28, 29, 30
    Dock menu options in the Dock itself, 35
    double-pointy symbol in, 30
    Finder icon in, 28

hide or show the Dock, 35
icon jumps up and down, 34
indicator lights in Dock, 30, 111
Launchpad icon in, 28
magnify individual icons, 33, 35
Mail icon in Dock has a number, 152
minimize windows down to Dock, 47
name of icon in Dock, how to see it, 30
open Dock icon menus, 21, 53
printer icon has a symbol on it, 103
rearrange items in the Dock, 31
remove items from the Dock, 31
reposition the Dock, 34
resize the Dock, 30, 33
Safari icon in Dock, 130
shortcut to quit applications, 113
springy-thing icon in Dock, 139
web page link, add to Dock, 139

documents
what are they? 1
analogy of typewriter and paper, 108
close a document, 108, 110
contextual menu for, 57
document window, 84
duplicate, make a copy, 91–92
"Edited" in title bar, 90, 109
New versus Open, 65
open a blank document to work in, 65
save your document with a name, 88–89
unsaved changes, visual clue for, 109
versions of, browse and open them, 90–91

Documents folder
in Favorites in the Sidebar, 5
in Dock, 29

double-click, 19–20

Downloads folder
in Dock, 29
in Favorites in Sidebar, 5
saves files from AirDrop, 181

duplicate a document, 91–92

DVDs, CDs
burn a disk, 180
open to see what is on the disk, 19

"Edited" in title bar, 90, 109
ellipsis (…)
how to type it, 201
in a menu, what it means, 56
email accounts. *See also* **Mail.**
email address, what it looks like, 147
IMAP or POP, 124, 146
incoming mail server name, 123, 147
outgoing mail server name, 123
SMTP, 123–124, 147
where to get an email account, 120
esc, Escape key
what is it and where is it? 6
force quit with, 113
keyboard symbol for, 58
Ethernet port, 121
euro symbol, how to type it, 83, 201
Exchange, set it up in Mail, 146
Exposé
manage windows with, 186–188
preferences for, 184

FaceTime
icon in Dock, what is it? 28
contact someone via Address Book, 165
fax from your Mac, 121
files
what is a file? 1
save a file in a different format, 89
Finder
what is it? 2
Desktop is run by the Finder, 2
Finder is active when a Finder window
is open, 38
icon in Dock, 15, 21, 39
Relaunch the Finder, 113
switch between Finder and application,
110–111

Finder windows
what are they? 2, 4–5, 38
how to work with Finder windows, 37–50
active windows, what are they? 38, 111
"Arrange by" menu and options, 41, 43, 49
Back and Forward buttons, 40
clean up the icons, 49
close a Finder window
close all windows at once, 59
with a keyboard shortcut, 59
with red close button, 18
Column View, 42–43
Cover Flow View, 44
document windows are different, 84
green button in, 18, 46
Icon View of, 39
List View in, 40–41
many open windows, manage them
with Exposé, 186–188
minimize windows to Dock, 47
open a Finder window
with a keyboard shortcut, 59
with a single click, 15, 39
preview file when in Column View, 42–43
red button in, 18, 46
reposition text labels in, 49
resize a window, 22, 46
resize columns
in Column View, 43
in List View, 41
*can't resize when an arrangement
is applied,* 41
resize icons in window, 49
resize text labels in window, 49
Sidebar in, 15, 16, 38
hide or show the Sidebar, 18
Status Bar in, hide or show it, 18, 39
title bar in, 16, 38
Toolbar in
where is the Toolbar? 38
"Arrange by" menu in Toolbar, 41, 43, 49
Back and Forward buttons, 40
hide or show the Toolbar, 18
View buttons in, 39

View Options for, 49
views of
change the view, 17, 39
Column View, 42–43
Cover Flow View, 44
Icon View of, 39
List View, 40–41
overview of options, 39–43
View Options for, 49
yellow button in, 18, 46

Fkeys
what and where is it? 6
keyboard symbols for, 58

fn key
what is it? 6
where is it? 11
use in combination with F9, 183

folders
what are they? 1
add or remove files from folders, 48
create your own, 48
double-click to open, 20
rename a folder, 48
Sidebar items are actually folders, 4

force quit an application, 25, 35, 113

full-screen apps, full-screen mode
apps occupy their own Spaces, 183, 185
as part of Mission Control, 182–187
get out of full-screen mode, 3, 185

G

gestures
in Mission Control, 183
on a Magic Mouse
or multi-touch trackpad, 13

Get Info window, 175

gigabyte, 108

Google
Google.com, 141
set up Gmail, calendar, and other accounts,
146

gray commands in a menu, 54

green button in upper-left of windows, 46

H

Hall, Lavonne, 166
Haney, Brianna Nora, 178
hard disk
    contextual menu for, 57
    open a disk to see what's on it, 19
hierarchical menus, 55
highlight. *See also* **select.**
    examples of highlighted files, 115
    highlighted text, 72
h-menus, 55
Home folders, where are they? 2
hot corners, 184
hover to make tooltips appear, 24, 30
hypertext links, 130

I

I-beam, 66
iCal
    what is it? 28
    calendar settings, set up in Mail, 146
iChat
    green orb in Mail, 155
    not explained in this book, 29
    photo from Address Book appears
        in iChat, 163
icons
    what are they? 1
    resize icons in a window, 39, 49
    resize icons in the Dock, 30, 33
    select with a single click, 15
Icon View of Finder windows, 39
IMAP account, 124
indicator lights in Dock, 30, 111
insertion point, 66–67
Internet, get connected, 119–128
Internet Service Provider, 120–121
iPhoto
    add photos to contacts in Address Book, 163
    add photos to email, 159
    not explained in this book, 29
    use image from as Desktop background, 171
ISP, 120–121
iTunes, 29

J

justified text, 75

K

keyboard
    modifier keys explained, 58
    special keys on the keyboard, 6
    wired keyboard stops working? 35
keyboard shortcuts, 58–59
    to use Exposé, 186
    type a letter to select a file, 20, 64
    Close a window: Command W, 110
    Copy: Command C, 82
    Cut: Command X, 82
    Paste: Command V, 82
    Save: Command S, 90
    Undo: Command Z, 81, 82, 117
Keynote application, 29, 61
kilobyte, 108
Kodak prints, 29

L

labels, color-code your files, 62
laptop trackpad, how to use it, 11
Launchpad
    what is it? 28, 64
    icon in Dock, 28, 64
        if it's not in your Dock, 64
left-aligned text, 75
List View in Finder windows, 40–41
Log Out
    applications quit on Log Out, 114
    log out of your Mac, 179

M

The Mac is not a typewriter, 71

Magic Mouse. *See also* **mouse.**
    what is it? 10–11
    gestures using the Magic Mouse, 13
        in Mission Control, 13, 183
        scroll through a Finder window, 23

Mail
    accounts, email account, set it up, 146–149
    add contact info to Address Book, 164
    attachments, send and receive, 158–160
    Bcc a message, 153
    blue orb, 155
    Cc a message, 151
    check for messages, 152
    Conversations
        how to work with them, 156–157
        delete one, delete them all, 157
    date, organize messages by, 155
    Dock icon has a number, 152
    download attachments from email, 160
    email address, how to write it, 150
    format a message, 153
    forward a message, 154
    green orb, 155
    HTML messages, 151
    icons in Mail
        delete icon, 149
        Forward this message, 149
        New Message icon, 149
        Reply, Reply All, 149
    listen to your message read aloud, 167
    Message List, what is it? 155, 156
    Message Pane
        what is it? 155, 156
        number in message, 156
        photos display in, 149
    Notes feature, 161
    open email message in separate window,
        149
    photos
        sender photos appear in Message Pane,
          149
        send photos through email, 158–159
    preferences you can change
        how often to check for mail, 149
        number of lines that show in the
          Message List, 149
        text labels under toolbar icons, 149

read your email, 149
reply to messages, 152, 154
save as draft, 153
search in Spotlight, 177
Sidebar
    hide or show it, 155
    in typical Mail layout, 156
stationery, fancy email, 151
Toolbar, view text labels under icons, 149
unread messages
    blue orb indicates unread, 155
    visual clue in Dock icon, 152
Viewer window in
    explained, 149
    customize the Viewer window, 155
write a message, 150–151
    address it using Address Book pane, 165
    Bcc message, 153
    Cc a message, 151
    format the message, 153
    save as drafts, 153

Mail, Contacts & Calendars preferences, 146

McDonald, Nikki, iv, 156–157

McMillin, Carla and Jamie, 161

megabyte, 108

memory
    apps and how they work in memory, 108
    how much does your Mac have? 108

menu bar, what and where is it? 2, 3, 18

menus
    checkmark in menu, 55
    choose a command from a menu, 18, 52–53
    contextual menus, 57
    ellipsis after menu command, 56
    gray vs. black commands, 54
    hierarchical menus, 33, 55
    keyboard shortcuts in, 58–59
    put it away without choosing anything,
        18, 21, 52
    symbols in menus, 58
    toggle switches for menu items, 70
    visual clues in dialog boxes, 60

Microsoft
    Exchange calendar, set it up, 146–149
    Microsoft Word
        save a TextEdit file as a Word doc, 89
        use Word just like TextEdit, 63–86

Mission Control, 182–188
    example of screen, 182
    experiment with gestures to open, 13
    preferences for, 184
MobileMe, 146
modem, 120–121
modifier keys, 58–59
mouse
    how to use it, 10–11
    double-click with, 19–20
    hover to make tooltips appear, 24
    Magic Mouse
        what is it? 10–11
        gestures on a Magic Mouse, 13
    move the mouse while in action, 24
    press, 21
    press-and-drag, 22–23
    scroll through a Finder window, 23
    single-click with, 14–18
    two-button mouse, 10–11
        open contextual menus with, 57
        turn on secondary button, 170
    wired mouse or non–Multi-touch mouse
        how to scroll sideways, 23
        stops working, 35
mousepad, 10
Movies folder, 5
multiple users, 179
Music folder, 5

N

Network preferences, 124–127
The Non-Designer's Type Book, 71

O

one space after a period, 71
Option key
    what and where is it? 6
    keyboard symbol for, 58
    Option-click, Option-drag, how to, 25
    type accent marks with, 83

P

package, 57
Page Setup options, 96
PageUp and PageDown keys, symbols for, 58
paste text or a graphic
    cut-and-paste process, 80
    how to do it, 79
    keyboard shortcut, 82
Path Bar, show or hide it, 175
PDF, save a document as a PDF, 93, 98
Photo Booth
    what is it? 29
    add photos to Address Book, 163
    add photos to email, 159
photographs
    add to Address Book contacts, 163
    send through email, 158–159
    store and organize in iPhoto, 29
    take photos of yourself in Photo Booth, 29
    use as Desktop background, 171
Pictures folder, 5
pointer
    hot spot on the pointer, 12
    I-beam is another pointer, 66–67
    move the pointer with the mouse or
        trackpad, 10–11
POP account, 124
pound sign (British), how to type it, 201
press-and-drag, 22–23
press with the mouse or trackpad, 21
previews
    files in Finder windows, 42
    in Preview application, 84
    of a job before it prints, 98
    Quick Look previews, 44

printing
> how to print your document, 93
> add a printer to print to, 94–95
> application-specific options, 97–98
> Dock printer icon
>> *printer icon has a symbol on it,* 103
>> *put icon in Dock permanently,* 105
>> *use its menu to resume printing,* 104
> exclamation point in printer name, 103
> install the software, 94
> mailing labels, envelopes, 98
> more than one page per sheet, 100
> orientation of paper, 96
> Page Setup options, 96
> paper makes a big difference, 101
> preview before printing, 98
> printer-specific settings, 101
> queue jobs for printing later, 102–104
> resume printing after a pause, 104
> select pages to print, 99
> two-sided, 100

provider. *See* **Internet Service Provider**
Put Back command, 117

Quick Look to view previews, 44
Quit
> applications
>> *how to quit,* 112
>> *when to quit,* 113
> automatically on Log Out, Restart,
>> Shut Down, 114
> Close versus Quit, 108
> force the application to quit, 35, 113
> how to quit if there is no menu, 3, 13
> keyboard shortcut for, 112
> menu item, how to find it, 3
> "Quit" is not in menu, 3, 112
> save changes on quitting, 112
> shortcut in Dock to quit, 113

RAM, 108
Recent files, display on screen, 186–188
red button in upper-left of windows, 46
red dots under words, 69
registration symbol, how to type one, 201
resize
> columns in List View, 41
> Dock
>> *magnify icons in the Dock,* 33
>> *resize the entire Dock,* 30
> Finder windows, 22, 46
> icons in Finder windows, 39, 49
> size of text labels in windows, 49
> text on web pages, 132

restart
> applications quit on restart, 114
> restart your Mac, 179

right-aligned text, 75
Rule Number One, 88, 109
Rule Number Two, 54, 74–75

S

Safari
    browser, use Safari, 129
    back and forward buttons, 133, 134
    bookmarks in, create and organize, 138–139
    Dock icon
        pop-up menu to choose pages, 134
        Safari icon, 130
    enter a web address, 135
    eyeglasses icon in Bookmarks Bar, 143
    Google.com, search with, 141
    History menu, 133
    Home button in toolbar, 137
    Home page, set your own, 137
    hypertext links, 130
    links on web pages, how to use, 131–132
    Reader mode, 142
    Reading List in, 143
    resize text on web pages, 132
    search web pages, 140 141
    Top Sites window, 140
    URL, 130, 136
    web address, 130, 136
    web pages, 130
        add links to Dock, 139
        open more than one, 134
Save As dialog box, 88–89
save your files
    "Edited" in title bar, 90, 109
    how to save, 88–89
    on quitting, 112
    versions, save various versions
        automatically, 90–91
screen saver preferences, 171
scroll bars
    Finder window, how to use them, 23
    turn them on always, 170
search
    search your Mac for files, 174–177
    search web pages, 140–141
select
    more than one file or icon, 25, 115
    select before applying a change, 74
    text in any application, 72–73, 75
        deselect text, 73
    "Select first, then do it to it", 54, 74–75
The Shakespeare Papers, 131
sheets as dialog boxes, 56

Shift key, 6
    keyboard symbol for, 58
    select text with Click Shift-Click, 73
    Shift-click, Shift-drag, how to, 25
Shut Down
    applications quit on Shut Down, 114
    Shut Down your Mac, 179
Sidebar
    add or remove items from, 45
    in a Finder window, 4
        Sidebar disappeared, how to get it back,
          4
single-click, 14–18
Sleep your Mac, 179
Slideshow previews, 44
SMTP, 123–124, 147
SOS: Save Often, Sweetie
    Rule Number One, 88, 109
Spacebar
    what is it? 6
    open Quick Look or a Slideshow, 44
Spaces
    add a new Space, 185
    Dashboard, 183, 187
        remove Dashboard from a Space, 184
    remove a Space, 185
special characters
    how to type them, 82–83
    list of accent marks, 202–203
    list of special characters, 201
spell checking, 69–70
Spotlight to search your Mac, 174–177
Status Bar, hide or show it, 18, 39
Stickies, 178
symbols
    in menus, 58–59
    on keyboard, 6
        cloverleaf symbol, 25
    to enter in text (copyright, British pound,
        cents, etc.), 82–83, 201
    triangles
        in List View in Finder window, 40
        disclosure triangles in dialog box, 89
        on a button in a dialog box, 60

System Preferences
how to access and use them, 170–171
icon in Dock, 170
specific preferences
Dashboard (widgets), 184
Desktop & Screen Saver, 171
Dock, 47
Exposé, 184
General, 170
Mail, Contacts & Calendars, 146
Mission Control, 184
Mouse, 57, 170
Network, 124–127
Print & Scan, 94–95, 105
Users & Groups, 179

TextEdit
how to use it, 63–86
add space between the lines
or between the paragraphs, 71
alignment of text, 75
Clear, same as Delete, 82
Clipboard, 76, 82
close a document, 110
copy text or a graphic, 76, 78
paste what you copied, 79
cut text or a graphic, 76–77
cut-and-paste process, 80
paste what you cut, 79
Delete versus Clear, 82
"Edited" in title bar, 90, 109
fonts, change typeface and/or size, 74
formatting tools in Toolbar, 74
grammar check, 70
I-beam, another pointer, 66–67
icon might not be in the Dock, 29, 32
insertion point, importance of, 66–67
one space after a period, 71
paragraphs, a new one starts with
every Return, 80
paste what you cut or copied, 79
PDF, save a document as, 93, 98
print a document, 93, 97–101
put TextEdit icon in the Dock, 32

quit TextEdit, how to, 113
Recent files, display on screen, 186–188
red dots under words, 69
remove a Return, 85
replace selected text, 73
save your document, 88–92
save regularly with a shortcut, 90
search in Spotlight, 177
set defaults for future documents, 70
spell checking, 69–70
typing
double-spaced document, 85
when to hit Return at the end of a line,
65
typos, how to fix them, 68–69
versions of a document, 90–92
Wrap to Page or Wrap to Window, 65

Tilde key, 6

title bar
where is it? 4
what it tells you, 16

toggle switches for menu items, 70

Tollett, John, ii, iv

tooltips
make them appear, 24, 30
misspelled words, 69

trackpad
how to use it, 11
double-click on it, 19–20
gestures on a Multi-Touch trackpad, 13
in Mission Control, 183
scroll through a Finder window, 23
hover to make tooltips appear, 24
press-and-drag on it, 22–23
press on it, 21
single-click on it, 14–18

trademark symbol, how to type it, 201

Trash
how to use it, 115–117
empty the Trash, 116
exercise in trashing files, 116
how to get items back after emptying
the Trash, 116
keyboard shortcuts to delete files, 116
paper is in Trash, 115
Put Back command, 117
remove item from Trash, 117
shortcuts to send items to Trash, 116
window for trashed items, 117

troubleshooting
  accidentally deleted something from the
    Dock, put it back in, 32
  cannot resize or move columns
    in Finder window, 41
  cut something and you want it back, 77
  Dock
    Dock has disappeared, 35
    icons jump up and down, 34
  double-click isn't working, 19
  everything is in ALL CAPS, 7
  force an application to quit, 25, 35, 113
  Help button on dialog boxes, 96
  Internet connection, set the service order,
    127
  keyboard stops working, 35
  margins are missing from TextEdit page, 65
  monitor has gone black, 7
  mouse
    click makes weird things happen, 11
    runs out of room, 24
    second button won't work, 57
    stops working, 35
  printing, document doesn't print, 103
  Quit
    is not in menu, 112
    app is acting stupid,
      must force it to quit, 35, 113
  relaunch the Finder, 113
  screen, monitor has gone black, 7
  scroll sideways with a mouse that does
    not have multi-touch, 23
  Sidebar in Finder window disappeared, 18
  things just happen
    all my windows disappeared, 186
    thumbnail pictures appear at the top
      of the screen, 185
    when my cursor gets close to a corner
      (hot corners), 184
  Toolbar in Finder window disappeared, 18
  trackpad makes you crazy, add a mouse, 11
two-button mouse
  if the second button isn't working, 57
  open contextual menus with it, 57
typing in a word processor. *See* **TextEdit.**

Undo, 81, 117
URL, 130. *See also* **web addresses.**
  explanation of URL, 136
USB port, 121
Utilities folder, 20

V

Van Ness, David, ii, iv
versions of documents, browse
    and open them, 90–91
View Options, 49, 61
visual clues
  arrows and triangles to indicate menus, 60
  blue highlight on icon name, 15
  Dock icons jump up and down, 34
  "Edited" in title bar, 90
  I-beam indicates where typing starts, 66
  of icons, 1
  of scroll bars, 22, 170
  paper in the Trash, 115
  red dots under words, 178
  web links, 131
VoiceOver, 170

web, web browser. *See* **Safari.**
Welles, Winifred, 77
West, Sarah, 164
widgets, 187
Williams family
  Brianna Nora Haney, 178
  Florence Weber, 44, 84
  Floyd Williams, 92
  Gerald Williams, iii, 43, 44, 92
  Jean Williams, 165
  Jeffrey Williams, 92
  Jewels Williams, 44
  Jimmy Thomas Williams, 151
  John Dorfer, 159
  Merv Williams, 92
  Patricia Williams, iii
  Ryan Williams, 143, 156–157
  Scarlett Williams, 159

windows. *See* **Finder windows.**
wireless Internet connection, 121
Word
    save a TextEdit file as a Word doc, 89
    save a TextEdit file as a Word doc, 89
    use Word just like TextEdit, 63–86
word processor
    accent marks, chart of, 202–203
    TextEdit, how to use it, 64–86

Y

Yahoo calendar, set it up, 146
yellow button in upper-left of windows, 47

Z

Zoom button, 46

Colophon

I wrote, designed, and did the layout, production, and index of this book in Adobe InDesign on my Mac. The body copy font is *Adobe Warnock Pro,* the sans serif is *Brandon Grotesque.* The abstract graphic elements in the chapter openers and closers are by John Tollett.

Special characters

The following is a list of the most often-used **special characters.** Remember, hold down the "modifier keys," the ones that don't do anything by themselves, then tap the character key just once.

"	Option [	opening double quote
"	Option Shift [	closing double quote
'	Option]	opening single quote
'	Option Shift]	closing single quote; apostrophe
–	Option Hyphen	en dash
—	Option Shift Hyphen	em dash
...	Option ;	ellipsis *(this character can't be separated at the end of a line as three periods can)*
•	Option 8	bullet *(easy to remember because it's the asterisk key)*
fi	Option Shift 5	ligature of f and i
fl	Option Shift 6	ligature of f and l
©	Option g	
™	Option 2	
®	Option r	
°	Option Shift 8	degree symbol (e.g., 102°F)
¢	Option $	
€	Option Shift 2	Euro symbol
/	Option Shift 1 (one)	fraction bar *(this doesn't descend below the line like the slash does)*
¡	Option 1 (one)	
¿	Option Shift ?	
£	Option 3	
ç	Option c	
Ç	Option Shift c	

Remember, to set an **accent mark** over a letter, press the Option key and the letter (it will look like nothing happened), then press the letter you want under it (see page 83). A complete chart is on the next two pages.

´	Option e
`	Option ~ (upper-left or next to the Spacebar)
¨	Option u
~	Option n
^	Option i

Accent marks

See page 83 if you're not sure how to type accent marks.

When you type some of these in Microsoft Word, the tops of the accent marks may appear to be cut off. They should print fine, though.

Tilde	Press	Let go, then press
~	Option n	Spacebar
ã	Option n	a
Ã	Option n	Shift a
ñ	Option n	n
Ñ	Option n	Shift n
õ	Option n	o
Õ	Option n	Shift o

Diaeresis	Press	Let go, then press
··	Option u	Spacebar
ä	Option u	a
Ä	Option u	Shift a
ë	Option u	e
Ë	Option u	Shift e
ï	Option u	i
Ï	Option Shift f	
ö	Option u	o
Ö	Option u	Shift o
ü	Option u	u
Ü	Option u	Shift u
ÿ	Option u	y

Circumflex	Press	Let go, then press
^	Option i	Spacebar
â	Option i	a
Â	Option Shift m	
ê	Option i	e
Ê	Option i	Shift e
î	Option i	i
Î	Option Shift d	
ô	Option i	o
Ô	Option Shift j	
û	Option i	u
Û	Option i	Shift u

Acute	Press	Let go, then press
´	Option e	Spacebar
á	Option e	a
Á	Option e *or* Option Shift y	Shift a
é	Option e	e
É	Option e	Shift e
í	Option e	i
Í	Option e *or* Option Shift s	Shift i
ó	Option e	o
Ó	Option e *or* Option Shift h	Shift o
ú	Option e	u
Ú	Option e *or* Option Shift ;	Shift u

Grave	Press	Let go, then press
`	Option `   (` is next to 1, or next to Spacebar; the same key as the regular ~ key)	Spacebar
à	Option `	a
À	Option `	Shift a
è	Option `	e
È	Option `	Shift e
ì	Option `	i
Ì	Option `	Shift i
ò	Option `	o
Ò	Option ` *or* Option Shift l (letter el)	Shift o
ù	Option `	u
Ù	Option `	Shift u

Miscellaneous	Press
å	Option a
Å	Option Shift a
ç	Option c
Ç	Option Shift c